PU

The Puffin Book of Nonsense Stories

Quentin Blake is one of Britain's most renowned illustrators. Born in the suburbs of London in 1932, he read English at Cambridge before becoming a full-time freelance illustrator. He began his career working for magazines such as *The Spectator* and *Punch*.

With a few deft, instantly recognizable strokes of the pen, Quentin Blake can animate any character or situation. His genius for illustration and sharp eye for humorous detail led him into the world of children's books, where he is respected and loved internationally for both his own picture books and collaborations with other authors. The first of these was with John Yeoman; some twenty books and thirty years later, their ingenuity and sense of mischief show no sign of flagging. The creative relationship between Quentin Blake and Roald Dahl was a particularly special and enduring one – his interpretation of Dahl's characters has become an integral part of childhood.

Quentin Blake was head of the Illustration Department at the Royal College of Art from 1978 to 1986 and is now a visiting Professor. He was awarded the OBE in 1988.

THE
PUFFIN BOOK
OF
NONSENSE
STORIES

SELECTED AND ILLUSTRATED BY

PUFFIN BOOKS

To Barny and Linda

PUFFIN BOOKS

Published by the Penguin Group
Penguin Books Ltd, 27 Wrights Lane, London W8 5TZ, England
Penguin Books USA Inc., 375 Hudson Street, New York, New York 10014, USA
Penguin Books Australia Ltd, Ringwood, Victoria, Australia
Penguin Books Canada Ltd, 10 Alcorn Avenue, Toronto, Ontario, Canada M4V 3B2
Penguin Books (NZ) Ltd, 182–190 Wairau Road, Auckland 10, New Zealand

Penguin Books Ltd, Registered Offices: Harmondsworth, Middlesex, England

First published by Viking 1996
Published in Puffin Books 1997
7

Filmset in Cochin

Made and printed in England by Clays Ltd, St Ives plc

British Library Cataloguing in Publication Data
A CIP catalogue record for this book is available from the British Library

ISBN 0–140–38213–5

CONTENTS

*I would like to express my
gratitude to Caroline Lederer for her work
on the translation of the French stories
in this collection.*

INTRODUCTION

A couple of years ago I was asked to put together a collection of nonsense verses and to illustrate them; this book is the result of an invitation to do the same sort of thing with nonsense stories.

It's a personal collection. In the first instance that means that I have not tried to make a judgement about the top thirty nonsense stories in the whole world or anything of that sort. This is just a collection of stories that appeal particularly to me. It's also a personal collection in the sense that I started off from the works of writers whose work I admire and, in many cases, have illustrated before: Joan Aiken, Russell Hoban, John Yeoman, Margaret Mahy, Clement Freud, J. P. Martin and Roald Dahl. In that respect it was rather like going to a party where you knew you were going to meet some of your friends. What was unusual about it, for me, was to have to make new pictures for these stories which I had previously illustrated in different ways at different times of my life – one or two quite recently, another as long as thirty years ago.

At the same time as gathering together these stories, so familiar to me, I have also tried to include extracts from some of the older classics of nonsense writing. In the middle of the book there's a piece of absolutely pure nonsense by Edward Lear, and at either end (like bookends, so to speak) are two chapters about Alice by Lewis Carroll. One is the Mad Hatter's Tea-party, perhaps the most famous nonsense situation ever described; the other is *The Wasp in a Wig* which was omitted from the published version of *Through the Looking Glass* and only came to light again within the last twenty years. Carroll's original illustrator was Sir John Tenniel, and the story is that this chapter was left out because he found it too difficult to draw. 'A wasp in a wig,' said Tenniel, 'is beyond the appliances of art.' This is rather odd, as he had already drawn a lot of things – a bread-and-butterfly, a sheep knitting – which you might have thought equally difficult. But I suspect that Tenniel was quite a serious-minded person, and perhaps his patience was exhausted.

Though Lear and Carroll were the two people who established nonsense as a recognized form of entertainment, they were not the first people to try their hand at it. There are, for instance, some wonderfully nonsensical moments in the writings, many years earlier, of a young person (nowadays we would call her a teenager) who later became a great novelist: Jane Austen. Lots of things she wrote for the amusement of her family were left unfinished, but *The Beautifull Cassandra*, though short, is complete. The Cassandra it is dedicated to was her beloved sister. It's interesting to note how similar Jane

Austen's sharp-eyed mischief is to Stephen Leacock's. Gertrude and Cassandra in the same story would be a striking combination.

I've also delved into another of my favourite books for another kind of nonsense: *Mark Twain's Library of Humor*. It was put together over a hundred years ago; and though Mark Twain's own humour wasn't for the most part about nonsense, many of his contributors were masters of that straight-faced, distinctively North American variety, the tall story. With those I've also included another, English, story (I've called it *Explosive in the Tree*) which also looks fairly tall. In fact, this isn't nonsense. It is, as is explained, true; and I suppose it could be called Life imitating Art.

The present book has one advantage that wasn't available to its predecessor. Nonsense poetry is extremely difficult to translate (though people have tried it, with varying degrees of success). Nonsense stories don't present the same problems, so that I have taken the opportunity of including stories from both France and Germany. I have had lots of entertainment reading Alphonse Allais, for instance, who was a very prolific contributor to the newspapers and humorous weeklies published in Paris at the beginning of the century. He had a taste for unexpected stories, and liked to explore slightly crazy variations on new scientific developments. He gave descriptions, for instance, of the Nonuplette, a nine-seater wickerwork cycle capable of extremely high speeds, and the Kangoocycle (an Australian idea, needless to say).

As I've been gathering these stories together over the past year I've also tried to decide what a nonsense story really *is*. In some respects it can't be quite as nonsensical as a poem, because it does tell a *story*, and that in its nature is a rather sensible kind of thing. But one thing I'm sure is essential: it should be shot through with a spirit of standing-things-on-their-heads, of mischief, of creative disorder.

But perhaps it is a pointless exercise to try and define the nature of the nonsense in this book. Perhaps I'd do better with a list of ingredients, as they do on packets and jars of things to eat. As it might be:

Contains: monster Christmas cracker, fried sausage, stifled lerch, itchy rhinoceros, obfustification, jellyhound, best butter, high explosive, Hitmouse, toast, sailor's hornpipe, zizzies, bottersnikes, rice pudding, wallpaper paste, Gondwana beasts, chyjeese knives, goldfish. . .

Could be delicious. I hope you like it.

A MAD TEA-PARTY

There was a table set out under a tree in front of the house, and the March Hare and the Hatter were having tea at it: a Dormouse was sitting between them, fast asleep, and the other two were resting their elbows on it, and talking over its head. 'Very uncomfortable for the Dormouse,' thought Alice; 'only, as it's asleep, I suppose it doesn't mind.'

The table was a large one, but the three were all crowded together at one corner of it. 'No room! No room!' they cried out when they saw Alice coming. 'There's *plenty* of room!' said Alice indignantly, and she sat down in a large arm-chair at one end of the table.

'Have some wine,' the March Hare said in an encouraging tone.

Alice looked all round the table, but there was nothing on it but tea. 'I don't see any wine,' she remarked.

'There isn't any,' said the March Hare.

'Then it wasn't very civil of you to offer it,' said Alice angrily.

'It wasn't very civil of you to sit down without being invited,' said the March Hare.

'I didn't know it was *your* table,' said Alice; 'it's laid for a great many more than three.'

'Your hair wants cutting,' said the Hatter. He had been looking at Alice for some time with great curiosity, and this was his first speech.

'You shouldn't make personal remarks,' Alice said with some severity; 'it's very rude.'

The Hatter opened his eyes very wide on hearing this; but all he *said* was 'Why is a raven like a writing-desk?'

'Come, we shall have some fun now!' thought Alice. 'I'm glad they've begun asking riddles. – I believe I can guess that,' she added aloud.

'Do you mean that you think you can find out the answer to it?' said the March Hare.

'Exactly so,' said Alice.

'Then you should say what you mean,' the March Hare went on.

'I do,' Alice hastily replied; 'at least – at least I mean what I say – that's the same thing, you know.'

'Not the same thing a bit!' said the Hatter. 'You might just as well say that "I see what I eat" is the same thing as "I eat what I see"!'

'You might just as well say,' added the March Hare, 'that "I like what I get" is the same thing as "I get what I like"!'

'You might just as well say,' added the Dormouse, who seemed to be talking in his sleep, 'that "I breathe when I sleep" is the same thing as "I sleep when I breathe"!'

'It *is* the same thing with you,' said the Hatter, and

here the conversation dropped, and the party sat silent for a minute while Alice thought over all she could remember about ravens and writing-desks, which wasn't much.

The Hatter was the first to break the silence. 'What day of the month is it?' he said, turning to Alice: he had taken his watch out of his pocket, and was looking at it uneasily, shaking it every now and then, and holding it to his ear.

Alice considered a little, and then said 'The fourth.'

'Two days wrong!' sighed the Hatter. 'I told you butter wouldn't suit the works!' he added, looking angrily at the March Hare.

'It was the *best* butter,' the March Hare meekly replied.

'Yes, but some crumbs must have got in as well,' the Hatter grumbled: 'you shouldn't have put it in with the bread-knife.'

The March Hare took the watch and looked at it gloomily: then he dipped it into his cup of tea, and looked at it again: but he could think of nothing better to say than his first remark, 'It was the *best* butter, you know.'

Alice had been looking over his shoulder with some curiosity. 'What a funny watch!' she remarked. 'It tells the day of the month, and doesn't tell what o'clock it is!'

'Why should it?' muttered the Hatter. 'Does *your* watch tell you what year it is?'

'Of course not,' Alice replied very readily: 'but that's because it stays the same year for such a long time together.'

'Which is just the case with *mine*,' said the Hatter.

Alice felt dreadfully puzzled. The Hatter's remark seemed to have no meaning in it, and yet it was certainly English. 'I don't quite understand,' she said, as politely as she could.

'The Dormouse is asleep again,' said the Hatter, and he poured a little hot tea upon its nose.

The Dormouse shook its head impatiently, and said, without opening its eyes, 'Of course, of course; just what I was going to remark myself.'

'Have you guessed the riddle yet?' the Hatter said, turning to Alice again.

'No, I give it up,' Alice replied: 'what's the answer?'

'I haven't the slightest idea,' said the Hatter.

'Nor I,' said the March Hare.

Alice sighed wearily. 'I think you might do something better with the time,' she said, 'than waste it asking riddles with no answers.'

'If you knew Time as well as I do,' said the Hatter, 'you wouldn't talk about wasting *it*. It's *him*.'

'I don't know what you mean,' said Alice.

'Of course you don't!' the Hatter said, tossing his head contemptuously. 'I dare say you never even spoke to Time!'

'Perhaps not,' Alice cautiously replied: 'but I know I

have to beat time when I learn music.'

'Ah! that accounts for it,' said the Hatter. 'He won't stand beating. Now, if you only kept on good terms with him, he'd do almost anything you liked with the clock. For instance, suppose it were nine o'clock in the morning, just time to begin lessons: you'd only have to whisper a hint to Time, and round goes the clock in a twinkling! Half-past one, time for dinner!'

('I only wish it was,' the March Hare said to itself in a whisper.)

'That would be grand, certainly,' said Alice thoughtfully: 'but then – I shouldn't be hungry for it, you know.'

'Not at first, perhaps,' said the Hatter: 'but you could keep it to half-past one as long as you liked.'

'Is that the way *you* manage?' Alice asked.

The Hatter shook his head mournfully. 'Not I!' he replied. 'We quarrelled last March – just before *he* went mad, you know –' (pointing with his teaspoon at the March Hare) '– it was at the great concert given by the Queen of Hearts, and I had to sing

> "*Twinkle, twinkle, little bat!*
> *How I wonder what you're at!*"

You know the song, perhaps?'

'I've heard something like it,' said Alice.

'It goes on, you know,' the Hatter continued, 'in this way:

> *"Up above the world you fly,*
> *Like a tea-tray in the sky.*
> *Twinkle, twinkle —"'*

Here the Dormouse shook itself, and began singing in its sleep 'Twinkle, twinkle, twinkle, twinkle —' and went on so long that they had to pinch it to make it stop.

'Well, I'd hardly finished the first verse,' said the Hatter, 'when the Queen jumped up and bawled out "He's murdering the time! Off with his head!"'

'How dreadfully savage!' exclaimed Alice.

'And ever since that,' the Hatter went on in a mournful tone, 'he won't do a thing I ask! It's always six o'clock now.'

A bright idea came into Alice's head. 'Is that the reason so many tea-things are put out here?' she asked.

'Yes, that's it,' said the Hatter with a sigh: 'it's always tea-time, and we've no time to wash the things between whiles.'

'Then you keep moving round, I suppose?' said Alice.

'Exactly so,' said the Hatter: 'as the things get used up.'

'But what happens when you come to the beginning again?' Alice ventured to ask.

'Suppose we change the subject,' the March Hare interrupted, yawning. 'I'm getting tired of this. I vote the young lady tells us a story.'

'I'm afraid I don't know one,' said Alice, rather alarmed at the proposal.

'Then the Dormouse shall!' they both cried. 'Wake up, Dormouse!' And they pinched it on both sides at once.

The Dormouse slowly opened his eyes. 'I wasn't asleep,' he said in a hoarse, feeble voice: 'I heard every word you fellows were saying.'

'Tell us a story!' said the March Hare.

'Yes, please do!' pleaded Alice.

'And be quick about it,' added the Hatter, 'or you'll be asleep again before it's done.'

'Once upon a time there were three little sisters,' the Dormouse began in a great hurry; 'and their names were Elsie, Lacie, and Tillie; and they lived at the bottom of a well –'

'What did they live on?' said Alice, who always took a great interest in questions of eating and drinking.

'They lived on treacle,' said the Dormouse, after thinking a minute or two.

'They couldn't have done that, you know,' Alice gently remarked; 'they'd have been ill.'

'So they were,' said the Dormouse; '*very* ill.'

Alice tried to fancy to herself what such an extraordinary way of living would be like, but it puzzled her too much, so she went on: 'But why did they live at the bottom of a well?'

'Take some more tea,' the March Hare said to Alice, very earnestly.

'I've had nothing yet,' Alice replied in an offended tone, 'so I can't take more.'

'You mean you can't take *less*,' said the Hatter: 'it's very easy to take *more* than nothing.'

'Nobody asked *your* opinion,' said Alice.

'Who's making personal remarks now?' the Hatter asked triumphantly.

Alice did not quite know what to say to this: so she helped herself to some tea and bread-and-butter, and then turned to the Dormouse, and repeated her question, 'Why did they live at the bottom of a well?'

The Dormouse again took a minute or two to think about it, and then said 'It was a treacle-well.'

'There's no such thing!' Alice was beginning very angrily, but the Hatter and the March Hare went 'Sh! sh!' and the Dormouse sulkily remarked, 'If you can't be civil, you'd better finish the story for yourself.'

'No, please go on!' Alice said. 'I won't interrupt again. I dare say there may be *one*.'

'One, indeed!' said the Dormouse indignantly. However, he consented to go on. 'And so these three little sisters – they were learning to draw, you know –'

'What did they draw?' said Alice, quite forgetting her promise.

'Treacle,' said the Dormouse, without considering at all this time.

'I want a clean cup,' interrupted the Hatter: 'let's all move one place on.'

He moved on as he spoke, and the Dormouse followed him: the March Hare moved into the Dormouse's place, and Alice rather unwillingly took the place of the March Hare. The Hatter was the only one who got any advantage from the change: and Alice was a good deal worse off, as the March Hare had just upset the milk-jug into his plate.

Alice did not wish to offend the Dormouse again, so she began very cautiously: 'But I don't understand. Where did they draw the treacle from?'

'You can draw water out of a water-well,' said the Hatter; 'so I should think you could draw treacle out of a treacle-well – eh, stupid?'

'But they were *in* the well,' Alice said to the Dormouse, not choosing to notice this last remark.

'Of course they were,' said the Dormouse; ' – well in.'

This answer so confused poor Alice, that she let the Dormouse go on for some time without interrupting it.

'They were learning to draw,' the Dormouse went on, yawning and rubbing its eyes, for it was getting very sleepy; 'and they drew all manner of things – everything that begins with an M –'

'Why with an M?' said Alice.

'Why not?' said the March Hare.

Alice was silent.

The Dormouse had closed its eyes by this time, and was going off into a doze; but, on being pinched by the Hatter, it woke up again with a little shriek, and went on: ' – that begins with an M, such as mouse-traps, and the moon, and memory, and muchness – you know you say things are "much of a muchness" – did you ever see such a thing as a drawing of a muchness?'

'Really, now you ask me,' said Alice, very much confused, 'I don't think –'

'Then you shouldn't talk,' said the Hatter.

This piece of rudeness was more than Alice could bear: she got up in great disgust, and walked off; the Dormouse fell asleep instantly, and neither of the others took the least notice of her going, though she looked back once or twice, half hoping that they would call after her: the last time she saw them, they were trying to put the Dormouse into the teapot.

'At any rate I'll never go *there* again!' said Alice as she picked her way through the wood. 'It's the stupidest tea-party I ever was at in all my life!'

FROM *ALICE'S ADVENTURES IN WONDERLAND*,
LEWIS CARROLL

SEVEN SHOPPING DAYS TO CHRISTMAS

Grimble's parents were very forgetful. This was some-times annoying, but having a forgetful father and mother also had advantages. For instance it meant that he had better bedtimes than most other children. Quite often he used to go into his father's room and say, 'I'm going to bed now; it's midnight'; and his father would say, 'Don't wait up for me' or 'Iquique is the only town I know with two qs!'

For most of the year Grimble – Grimble was his whole name, his parents had forgotten to give him any other names – rather enjoyed having a father and mother who were different from those of the other boys at school, but when it came to Christmas there were very definite disadvantages.

Grimble had only two more days of school before the Christmas holidays started – and the old Grimbles went around as if it were the middle of February or the end of August; anyway there was nothing special about the way they went around. The shops in the High Street had windows decorated with lights and Father Christmases and wrapped-up packages and mince pies and a big notice saying ONLY SEVEN MORE SHOPPING DAYS TO

CHRISTMAS on which the number of days before the twenty-fifth was changed every evening . . . it was very exciting.

And Grimble's mother went out with a big shopping bag – and came back with a cabbage, and one and a half pounds of cod fillets. I don't want to be unkind about cod fillets. They are perfectly all right but they just do not make you tingle all over. Anyway they didn't make Grimble tingle all over.

Grimble had a friend called David Sebastian Waghorn whose mother had said, 'We are going to have cold turkey on Boxing Day.' That is just about the same as saying, 'On Christmas Day, we are going to have hot roast turkey with stuffing and gravy and sausages and bacon and roast potatoes and Brussels sprouts.' He waited anxiously for Mrs Grimble to give some small hint like that. The evening before she had said, 'Have you put the cat out?' and Grimble said, 'We haven't got a cat,' and Mrs Grimble said, 'Oh dear, nor we have, don't forget to leave her a saucer of milk.'

Grimble watched his parents carefully for any sign that they might have remembered why he was going to be on holiday and when, and what sort of treats he was going to get if he was going to get treats. He worked hard giving them well-mannered hints because it was terribly important to him that Christmas would be, well . . . complete.

One evening he dropped a lot of pine needles on the

carpet ... but as no one noticed or said anything and Grimble was very tidy, he got a dust-pan and brush and swept them up again a couple of days later.

Also he tried to hum 'Good King Wenceslas' ... mm mmmmmmmm mm mmmmmm m, but he did not hum very well and his father, thinking it was 'God Save the Queen', stood up and when Grimble had finished humming his father turned off the television set and went to bed.

So he practised humming some more. David Sebastian Waghorn had a joke about humming. 'Do you know why humming birds hum? Because they don't know the words.' Grimble thought David Sebastian Waghorn was a very funny boy.

The day before, Mr Grimble had come into the house with a large square parcel and Grimble, knowing that it was not polite to be openly curious, had gone into the kitchen and watched his father take the parcel into the study through the slightly open door. It looked as if it might be a bicycle taken to pieces or a large box kite or possibly a new kind of cooker.

That evening his father said, 'Come into the study and see what I've got in my parcel. It's a footstool, I gave it to me . . .' and Grimble had clenched his teeth and said, 'Now you can lie back in your chair and don't even have to bend your legs.' His father was delighted that Grimble had got the point of the footstool so quickly and showed him where Iquique was on the globe of the world . . . it was about half-way down South America on the left-hand side.

'Do you expect to get anything else for Christmas . . . except for my presents . . .' he asked his father in an offhand way. 'A lot of weather,' said his father, who had just found Birmingham on the globe.

That night when Grimble was in bed he started to think about Christmas very seriously. Christmas was a holiday and a time for eating interesting food and giving presents and receiving presents – someone had told him that it was more blessed to do one than the other, but he kept forgetting which. Now the reason why children expected their parents to do things for them at Christmas was because parents are better organized than children and parents have more money than children.

In Grimble's case this was only partly true. His parents were not nearly as well organized as he; they kept forgetting to get up in the morning and sometimes forgot to go to bed for days on end and they never knew what time it was.

But the old Grimbles did have more money than he . . . or he hoped they did, because Grimble only had 19p and an Irish 5p piece. He lay in bed practising his humming and wondering whether, if one was really well organized, as he was – satchel packed; homework done; toothpaste squeezed out on to toothbrush; tie tied in a knot and opened out into a big loop so that it would go over his head; shoelaces done up so that he could step into his shoes and wriggle them about till the heels gave way . . . anyway, if someone were really well organized, it should not be very difficult for him to make money . . . and if he had money then he could arrange the whole family Christmas celebrations.

One evening Grimble had listened to a television

programme about money in which a man had said that the important thing was to find something that everyone needed. That way, you had a ready market for whatever you were going to sell . . . for instance the man explained: 'It is a better thing to go from house to house selling socks, which everyone wears, than suspenders – which are rubber straps that go round your leg below the knee and keep the socks up. Hardly anyone wears suspenders,' said the man. Grimble had never even heard of suspenders. 'Also,' said the man, 'you have to spend some of your money on getting people interested in your wares – this is called advertising.'

Grimble was very impressed and wrote a small note to remind himself: to sell successfully you have to find something everyone wants, and advertise it.

It was quite clear to Grimble that if a man wants to earn money by selling things, he would have to buy them first; the simple problem that Grimble had was what could he buy for 19p that he might be able to sell for a lot of money – because a turkey and a Christmas pudding and presents and everything would cost pounds. One of the masters at school had told them about an old Greek who was lying in a bathtub when an apple fell on his head and he shouted, 'Eureka, I've got it!' and invented gold, or something like that. Grimble lay in his bed thinking hard waiting to shout, 'Eureka, I've got it!' but he fell asleep.

In the morning he went to the shop on the corner and

as it was empty he looked carefully around for something that everyone needed that cost 19p or less. There were rolls of flypaper and some suntan cream and washing soap and tins of sardines and lemonade crystals. These were all dusty, which is a bad sign. Suddenly he saw a loaf of bread and a great idea occurred to him: everyone needed bread; if he went around selling bread slice by slice to people so that they wouldn't have to go to shops he could become very rich. And then he thought most people already have bread, but if I sold toast . . . not only sold it but took it to people just when they wanted it. When they were sitting at the breakfast table with butter

on the knife and a marmalade jar in front of them ...
the GRIMBLE HOME TOAST DELIVERY SERVICE. Proprietor
Grimble. 'Eureka, I've got it!' he shouted and the old
lady came out from the back of the shop and said, 'If
you've got it you'd better pay for it. That is the only way
you can do things in a shop.'

Grimble was much too excited to explain, so he paid
the lady 6p which was the price of that loaf of bread and
went to school.

He didn't learn much at school that day because he
was working out his toast business. The loaf of bread
was in his locker; it was a cut loaf called THIN SLICED
which seemed a silly name to give a loaf and it contained
eighteen pieces of bread wrapped in greaseproof paper.
(If the business really succeeds, he thought, I might go
into the greaseproof-paper business.)

Every morning nearly everyone eats toast and, as toast
is quite boring to make, Grimble decided that if he made
toast at seven every morning and brought it to people
all hot and ready they would definitely pay $2\frac{1}{2}$p for three
slices, which meant six times three slices in a loaf which
is 15p back for 6p.

When he came home from school he sat down at his
desk and got a large piece of paper and cut it in half and
then cut each half into half again and then halved the
four pieces of paper so that he had eight small pieces
and on each one he wrote the message THE GRIMBLE HOME
TOAST DELIVERY SERVICE PROPRIETOR GRIMBLE founded

1974. On the other side he wrote: Toast delivered, daily, tidily, un-burntly, punctually. 2½p for three slices. Our representative will call tomorrow morning with a free slice and awaits the pleasure of your order.

He took the eight pieces of paper and put four of them through the letter boxes of the four houses up the hill from his house and posted the other four through the doors on the downhill side. As he was going back home he decided that as he did not know a great deal about toast he had better go and see Madame Beryl, who was a fat kind friend of his mother's who kept a bakery shop and knew a lot about things like that.

'Good afternoon,' said Grimble, entering the shop. 'I would like to have a small discussion with you about bread.' 'I prefer,' said Madame Beryl, 'to talk about cake.' 'I meant to say toast,' said Grimble. 'I still meant cake,' said Madame Beryl. She eased her right foot out of her shoe, which came away with a small sigh of relief, and said, 'I would very much like to talk to you about bread AND toast but unfortunately I have to go and see a man about a wedding breakfast. Can it wait until after Christmas?'

'I am afraid,' said Grimble, 'that after Christmas will be exactly too late.' There was a small silence. 'I have done a very silly thing,' said Madame Beryl. 'I baked a cake which had not been ordered and now I don't know what to do with it and the dustbin is full. Do you think you would be very kind and take possession of it?' 'Oh, yes, thank you,' said Grimble, 'if it is really in your way.' And Madame Beryl put her foot back into her protesting shoe, got a quite large cake, gave it to Grimble, said, 'Oh dear, I must fly,' and started moving into the street like a cabin trunk. 'About toast,' said Grimble following her. 'Not toast,' puffed Madame Beryl. 'Never toast cake. Ice it with icing sugar and egg white,' and she waddled on to a bus.

Grimble found himself alone with a cake and then he thought, actually a cake with icing is a very Christmassy thing to have and tomorrow I shall start up my business and in nine days' time it will be Christmas Eve and even if my parents have forgotten, it's going to be an absolutely complete proper well-organized Christmas.

FROM *GRIMBLE AT CHRISTMAS*,
CLEMENT FREUD

CHRISTMAS AT AUNT FIDGET WONKHAM-STRONG'S

At Christmas Tom gave Aunt Fidget Wonkham-Strong a new iron hat and she gave him a sledge.

'What's that wrapped round the runners?' said Tom.

'Sackcloth,' said Aunt Fidget. 'So you won't go down the hill too fast. I don't want you shooting off the bank and into the river.'

'There's ice on the river,' said Tom.

'Yes, but it's thin ice,' said Aunt Fidget. 'So keep your sackcloth on. You may have three goes and then you must come in for dinner.'

'What are we having?' said Tom.

'Stifled lerch with boiled lumbrage and mashed thung,' said Aunt Fidget, 'and there's ploddy-groan for pudding. Hurry with your sledging now, dinner's almost ready.'

Tom leapt on to his sledge but the sledge did not move. 'Silly to have to pull it *both* ways,' said Tom. He took the sackcloth off the runners and down the hill he went.

The sledge was moving fast, and Tom was just about to shoot off the riverbank when he saw something coming up through the ice in front of him. It was Captain Najork's head. The Captain was trying out the diving gear Aunt Fidget Wonkham-Strong had given him for Christmas.

Tom swerved sharply and the sledge hit a stump but he kept going. He shot across the river like a cannonball and knocked down the Headmistress of the girls' school.

She was just about to have a nude swim with the ladies of the Polar Bare Club. 'Help!' she screamed as she caught Tom.

'Coming!' shouted Captain Najork from across the river. He came gliding under the ice like a seal and he surfaced among the nude ladies.

'Another one!' screamed the ladies. 'This one's all in black rubber!'

'Pervert!' said the Headmistress. With one hand she fired Tom back across the river while with the other she grabbed Captain Najork by the snorkel.

At that moment Aunt Fidget Wonkham-Strong was coming down the hill in her wet suit. From the observatory she had seen Captain Najork being roughly handled by the nude ladies and she thought he might need help. 'Hang on!' she shouted to him, 'I shan't be a moment!' She was just putting on her flippers when Tom came hurtling through the air and knocked her senseless.

Aunt Fidget woke up in her bed. Tom and Captain Najork were bending anxiously over her. 'Are you all right, my dear?' said the Captain.

'I'll have a word to you later,' said Aunt Fidget. To Tom she said, 'What do you mean by flying at me like that?'

'I was thrown,' said Tom.

'I told you to keep your sackcloth on,' said Aunt Fidget.

'We've brought you up a tray,' said Captain Najork. 'Sit up and eat your lerch before it gets cold.'

'Thank you,' said Aunt Fidget. 'It *is* a festive-looking dish, isn't it?'

'It is,' said Captain Najork. 'And I've poured a little brandy over the ploddy-groan. Happy Christmas!'

'Happy Christmas, Aunt Fidget!' said Tom.

'Happy Christmas, all!' said Aunt Fidget, and ate her stifled lerch.

RUSSELL HOBAN

VIOLET AND THE CHEWING-GUM

Mr Wonka led the party over to a gigantic machine that stood in the very centre of the Inventing Room. It was a mountain of gleaming metal that towered high above the children and their parents. Out of the very top of it there sprouted hundreds and hundreds of thin glass tubes, and the glass tubes all curled downwards and came together in a bunch and hung suspended over an enormous round tub as big as a bath.

'Here we go!' cried Mr Wonka, and he pressed three different buttons on the side of the machine. A second later, a mighty rumbling sound came from inside it, and the whole machine began to shake most frighteningly, and steam began hissing out of it all over, and then suddenly the watchers noticed that runny stuff was pouring down the insides of all the hundreds of little glass tubes and squirting out into the great tub below. And in every single tube the runny stuff was of a different colour, so that all the colours of the rainbow (and many others as well) came sloshing and splashing into the tub. It was a lovely sight. And when the tub was nearly full, Mr Wonka pressed another button, and immediately the runny stuff disappeared, and a whizzing whirring noise took its place; and then a giant whizzer started whizzing

round inside the enormous tub, mixing up all the different coloured liquids like an ice-cream soda. Gradually, the mixture began to froth. It became frothier and frothier, and it turned from blue to white to green to brown to yellow, then back to blue again.

'Watch!' said Mr Wonka.

Click went the machine, and the whizzer stopped whizzing. And now there came a sort of sucking noise, and very quickly all the blue frothy mixture in the huge basin was sucked back into the stomach of the machine. There was a moment of silence. Then a few queer rumblings were heard. Then silence again. Then suddenly, the machine let out a monstrous mighty groan, and at the same moment a tiny drawer (no bigger than the drawer in a slot machine) popped out of the side of the machine, and in the drawer there lay something so small and thin and grey that everyone thought it must be a mistake. The thing looked like a little strip of grey cardboard.

The children and their parents stared at the little grey strip lying in the drawer.

'You mean that's *all*?' said Mike Teavee, disgusted.

'That's all,' answered Mr Wonka, gazing proudly at the result. 'Don't you know what it is?'

There was a pause. Then suddenly, Violet Beauregarde, the silly gum-chewing girl, let out a yell of excitement. 'By gum, it's *gum*!' she shrieked. 'It's a stick of chewing-gum!'

'Right you are!' cried Mr Wonka, slapping Violet hard on the back. 'It's a stick of gum! It's a stick of the most *amazing* and *fabulous* and *sensational* gum in the world!' 'This gum,' Mr Wonka went on, 'is my latest, my greatest, my most fascinating invention! It's a chewing-gum meal! It's . . . it's . . . it's . . . That tiny little strip of gum lying there is a whole three-course dinner all by itself!'

'What sort of nonsense is this?' said one of the fathers.

'My dear sir!' cried Mr Wonka, 'when I start selling this gum in the shops it will change *everything*! It will be the end of all kitchens and all cooking! There will be no more shopping to do! No more buying of meat and groceries! There'll be no knives and forks at mealtimes! No plates! No washing up! No rubbish! No mess! Just a little strip of Wonka's magic chewing-gum – and that's all you'll ever need at breakfast, lunch, and supper! This piece of gum I've just made happens to be tomato soup, roast beef, and blueberry pie, but you can have almost anything you want!'

'What *do* you mean, it's tomato soup, roast beef, and blueberry pie?' said Violet Beauregarde.

'If you were to start chewing it,' said Mr Wonka, 'then that is exactly what you would get on the menu. It's absolutely amazing! You can actually *feel* the food going down your throat and into your tummy! And you can taste it perfectly! And it fills you up! It satisfies you! It's terrific!'

'It's utterly impossible,' said Veruca Salt.

'Just so long as it's gum,' shouted Violet Beauregarde, 'just so long as it's a piece of gum and I can chew it, then *that's* for me!' And quickly she took her own world-record piece of chewing-gum out of her mouth and stuck it behind her left ear.

'Come on, Mr Wonka,' she said, 'hand over this magic gum of yours and we'll see if the thing works.'

'Now, Violet,' said Mrs Beauregarde, her mother; 'don't let's do anything silly, Violet.'

'I want the gum!' Violet said obstinately. 'What's so silly?'

'I would rather you didn't take it,' Mr Wonka told her gently. 'You see, I haven't got it *quite right* yet. There are still one or two things . . .'

'Oh, to blazes with that!' said Violet, and suddenly, before Mr Wonka could stop her, she shot out a fat hand and grabbed the stick of gum out of the little drawer and popped it into her mouth. At once, her huge, well-trained jaws started chewing away on it like a pair of tongs.

'Don't!' said Mr Wonka.

'Fabulous!' shouted Violet. 'It's tomato soup! It's hot and creamy and delicious! I can feel it running down my throat!'

'Stop!' said Mr Wonka. 'The gum isn't ready yet! It's not right!'

'Of course it's right!' said Violet. 'It's working beautifully! Oh my, what lovely soup this is!'

'Spit it out!' said Mr Wonka.

'It's changing!' shouted Violet, chewing and grinning both at the same time. 'The second course is coming up! It's roast beef! It's tender and juicy! Oh boy, what a flavour! The baked potato is marvellous, too! It's got a crispy skin and it's all filled with butter inside!'

'But how *in*-teresting, Violet,' said Mrs Beauregarde. 'You are a clever girl.'

'Keep chewing, baby!' said Mr Beauregarde. 'Keep right on chewing! This is a great day for the Beauregardes! Our little girl is the first person in the world to have a chewing-gum meal!'

Everybody was watching Violet Beauregarde as she stood there chewing this extraordinary gum. Little Charlie Bucket was staring at her absolutely spellbound, watching her huge rubbery lips as they pressed and

unpressed with the chewing, and Grandpa Joe stood beside him, gaping at the girl. Mr Wonka was wringing his hands and saying, 'No, no, no, no, no! It isn't ready for eating! It isn't right! You mustn't do it!'

'Blueberry pie and cream!' shouted Violet. 'Here it comes! Oh my, it's perfect! It's beautiful! It's ... it's exactly as though I'm swallowing it! It's as though I'm chewing and swallowing great big spoonfuls of the most marvellous blueberry pie in the world!'

'Good heavens, girl!' shrieked Mrs Beauregarde suddenly, staring at Violet, 'what's happening to your nose!'

'Oh, be quiet, mother, and let me finish!' said Violet.

'It's turning blue!' screamed Mrs Beauregarde. 'Your nose is turning blue as a blueberry!'

'Your mother is right!' shouted Mr Beauregarde. 'Your whole nose has gone purple!'

'What *do* you mean?' said Violet, still chewing away.

'Your cheeks!' screamed Mrs Beauregarde. 'They're turning blue as well! So is your chin! Your whole face is turning blue!'

'Spit that gum out at once!' ordered Mr Beauregarde.

'Mercy! Save us!' yelled Mrs Beauregarde. 'The girl's going blue and purple all over! Even her hair is changing colour! Violet, you're turning violet, Violet! What *is* happening to you?'

'I *told* you I hadn't got it quite right,' sighed Mr Wonka, shaking his head sadly.

'I'll say you haven't!' cried Mrs Beauregarde. 'Just look at the girl now!'

Everybody was staring at Violet. And what a terrible, peculiar sight she was! Her face and hands and legs and neck, in fact the skin all over her body, as well as her great big mop of curly hair, had turned a brilliant, purplish-blue, the colour of blueberry juice!

'It always goes wrong when we come to the dessert,' sighed Mr Wonka. 'It's the blueberry pie that does it. But I'll get it right one day, you wait and see.'

'Violet,' screamed Mrs Beauregarde, 'you're swelling up!'

'I feel sick,' Violet said.

'You're swelling up!' screamed Mrs Beauregarde again.

'I feel most peculiar!' gasped Violet.

'I'm not surprised!' said Mr Beauregarde.

'Great heavens, girl!' screeched Mrs Beauregarde. 'You're blowing up like a balloon!'

'Like a blueberry,' said Mr Wonka.

'Call a doctor!' shouted Mr Beauregarde.

'Prick her with a pin!' said one of the other fathers.

'Save her!' cried Mrs Beauregarde, wringing her hands.

But there was no saving her now. Her body was swelling up and changing shape at such a rate that within a minute it had turned into nothing less than an enormous round blue ball – a gigantic blueberry, in fact – and all

that remained of Violet Beauregarde herself was a tiny pair of legs and a tiny pair of arms sticking out of the great round fruit and little head on top.

'It *always* happens like that,' sighed Mr Wonka. 'I've tried it twenty times in the Testing Room on twenty Oompa-Loompas, and every one of them finished up as a blueberry. It's most annoying. I just can't understand it.'

'But I don't want a blueberry for a daughter!' yelled Mrs Beauregarde. 'Put her back to what she was this instant!'

Mr Wonka clicked his fingers, and ten Oompa-Loompas appeared immediately at his side.

'Roll Miss Beauregarde into the boat,' he said to them, 'and take her along to the Juicing Room at once.'

'The *Juicing Room*?' cried Mrs Beauregarde. 'What are they going to do to her there?'

'Squeeze her,' said Mr Wonka. 'We've got to squeeze the juice out of her immediately. After that, we'll just have to see how she comes out. But don't worry, my dear Mrs Beauregarde. We'll get her repaired if it's the last thing we do. I am sorry about it all, I really am . . .'

FROM *CHARLIE AND THE CHOCOLATE FACTORY*,
ROALD DAHL

OLIVER TRIMBLE AND THE JELLY HOUND

In a village near the highest part of England there lived a boy made from raspberry jelly. He was named Oliver Trimble and his mother made him in a Waterford crystal jelly mould after she had produced six daughters one after the other.

Oliver was an unhappy baby and everybody thought it was because his sisters could not resist nibbling his toes and fingers, which tasted sweeter than figs in honey, but when he learned to talk he explained the real reason.

'I really wanted to be made from gooseberry jelly,' he said rather crossly.

'Proud Master Discontent!' cried his mother, furious at criticism of her jelly recipe. 'Gooseberry jelly indeed. Even the King is only his mother's son and must stay as he was born.'

Soft and slippery as Oliver was, his mother found him very hard to bring up. When she bathed him, using only the iciest water in case he dissolved, he shot from between her hands like a large and angry piece of soap. If she sat him on the kitchen table to put on his vest, and was called away by a knock at the door, he would slide off the table before you could say, 'Oh, my eye!' and start to melt in front of the big fire that always burns in kitchens in villages near the highest part of England.

Once, after he had just learned to walk, he slipped out of the house, wobbled down the street, went to splash in the rain-filled gutter and slid down between the gratings of a drain. It took the fire brigade, a plumber and a deep-sea diver to fish him out, and he turned into the oddest shape and had to go back into his mould for three days and nights.

He was not always naughty or discontented, however. He grew into a likeable lad and everybody said he had a most healthy complexion. But he did have his moods. He had to sleep in the icebox of the refrigerator and could not sit near the fire with his mother and sisters, playing snakes and ladders, which he loved. His school friends blamed him for their colds because the window beside his desk was left open on the most freezing days. You could not blame him for getting fed up.

They liked him on the whole, however, because at dinner-time he would let them see the food going down inside him. Watching pies and cakes and hard-boiled eggs float dreamily down to his stomach was always a popular notion. Once he swallowed a half-penny piece by mistake and the surgeon was able to see where it was without using an X-ray machine.

He hated the summer because he lost such a lot of weight. He attracted swarms of sweet-toothed wasps and little dogs ran up to lick him. And he hated birthday parties, because people always ate jelly. Eating jelly would have made him a cannibal, of course, and he couldn't stand cannibals. On his own birthdays the children who came to his parties were very kind and did not mention jelly, except for one very greedy boy named Ben, who was never asked again. Instead they had gallons of ice-cream and chocolate mousse.

Oliver loved winter best of all, because when the weather grew very cold his mother let him sleep on the lawn. It was heaven to lie under the inky sky and feel the snowflakes descending on him and to wake up tucked snugly in great white drifts. He liked making snowmen and holding long conversations with them, for he knew their language; but when the thaws came his heart would break to see his winter friends melting away with tears running swiftly and terribly down their shapeless faces. It made him shake like – like a leaf.

Then a most terrible thing happened. There was a great heatwave in England. Month after month the sun blazed down and no jellies would set. There was a nation-wide jelly famine.

Oliver Trimble fell so ill that he almost died, but his mother and six sisters travelled all over England and parts of the North Pole to find lumps of ice to tuck round him in the refrigerator. Even then, he almost slipped through their fingers.

Worst of all was that the King, who was fat and greedy, loved nothing better than jelly. He sent his soldiers to search every refrigerator in England and had big notices printed saying:

WANTED: (JELLIES ESPECIALLY RASPBERRY)

£1,000 REWARD

ANYBODY HIDING JELLIES WILL HAVE HIS

HEAD CUT OFF

One morning in June there was a mighty knock at the door and Oliver's mother opened it to find two of the King's fattest sergeant-majors standing there with an enormous gold barrel. They were so fat, and wore such heavy boots, that at every step they took the cobblestones were smashed to powder.

'We've come for Oliver Trimble,' said one of them, smacking his lips. 'Bring him out.'

'But he melted away long ago,' said Oliver's mother.

'Well pour him out,' said the second sergeant-major. 'Pour him into the King's giant jelly barrel.'

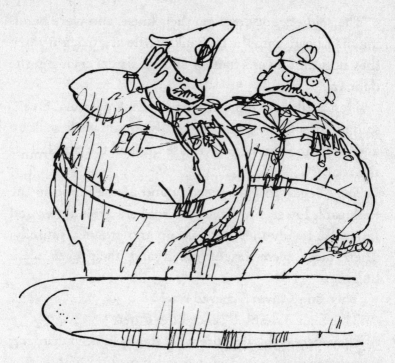

'But after he melted he evaporated,' said Mrs Trimble.

The sergeant-majors tramped past her into the house, stamping so hard that the plates fell off the Welsh dresser. They marched straight into the bathroom and cried, 'Oho! Oho!' so loudly that the tiles cracked and the lavatory flushed without the chain being pulled.

There in the bath lay a pool of raspberry-coloured liquid.

'How do you do, Oliver Trimble,' said the first sergeant-major, saluting the bathtub and clicking his heels. 'Pleased to eat you. I mean meet you.'

The soldiers got down on their knees and were bending their heads into the bath, like cattle at a trough, when they noticed Oliver's mother and six sisters crying in the doorway.

'Don't tell the King we've had a drink of your Oliver,' said the first fat sergeant-major. 'If you do we'll walk up and down in front of your house until all the tiles fall off the roof.'

They began to gulp greedily and as the liquid in the bath sank lower and lower the soldiers grew fatter and fatter. Suddenly they both sat up and groaned pitifully. Their faces were bright green and their eyes were bulging.

'This isn't Oliver!' roared one.

'This ain't Trimble!' roared the other.

They were right, because what they had been drinking was water dyed with red ink and mixed up with castor oil. Oliver's mother had put it there for just such a visit.

The two sergeant-majors ran out into the garden to be ill, looking very sheepish. Afterwards they were so cross that they walked up and down under the apple trees and made all the fruit tumble to the turf.

'We'll be back at twelve o'clock and you won't fool us again,' said the first soldier as they left. 'We'll bring the jelly hound.'

Oliver's mother and sisters shook with alarm at the mention of this fearful animal, which could stand on a cliff at Dover and smell a jelly in Calais.

At twelve o'clock there was an awful sniffling and snuffling at the door and the fat sergeant-majors, holding thick leather leashes with big metal studs, were dragged inside by the strangest beast you ever saw. It had hardly any body at all and was really just a gigantic, hairy, quivering nose standing on four legs. It stood in the kitchen for a moment with its trembling nose held high in the air, snuffering and snaffering, and then it took off and leapt through the air like a dolphin. It was an impressive sight, this huge, throbbing nose flying over the kitchen table with two fat sergeant-majors sailing behind. They landed in an untidy heap of nose, boots and elbows at the door of the refrigerator.

Mrs Trimble picked up her broom to attack the intruders, but the jelly hound gave a tremendous sniff and she was sucked up inside one of its nostrils so that only her feet were sticking out. The soldiers pulled her out by the ankles and said that if she ever did it again they would let the hound smell her away entirely.

Then they flung open the refrigerator door, pulled Oliver out, put him into the golden jelly barrel, packed him about with ice and took him away.

Seventy-six of the seventy-seven refrigerators at the King's palace had broken down with the overwork of cooling all the jellies his soldiers had discovered during the heatwave. The seventy-seventh was holding a jelly elephant and a jelly giraffe, so another place had to be found for Oliver. This was the royal bathroom, where there were two silver bathtubs, one for the King and one for the Queen.

As Oliver was slipped over the edge into one of the tubs he noticed that somebody else was lying in the other one. It was a beautiful gooseberry jelly girl named Grace Fullwobble. Oliver tried to talk to her but the bathroom was hot and her tongue had melted away. Soon she was just a lovely green pool; and shortly after that Oliver himself fell into a deep slumber and melted away.

The daylight melted away, too, and just as the night was at its blackest six pale little faces pressed themselves against the bathroom window, which had been left open a crack to keep the place cool. It was Oliver's six sisters.

Bethany, the eldest, put her hand inside to open the window wider. 'Oh, my dears!' she cried.

'What's the matter?' asked the other five.

'There are bars at the windows,' said Bethany. 'It's like a prison. We'll never, never get in. And – oh!'

For the door had suddenly opened and a giant of a man with a gold crown came into the bathroom, followed by one of the fat sergeant-majors.

'I'm so excited,' said the King, in a booming, rolling voice with a velvety edge that came of a pure diet of jelly. 'I'm all of a tremble.'

'No, you're King Horace,' said the fat sergeant-major. He pointed to the bathtub. 'That's Oliver Trimble. And that one over there's Grace Fullwobble.'

'I know I'm not Oliver Trimble,' the King said crossly. 'I said I'm all of a tremble.'

'Well, I suppose you know best,' said the fat sergeant-major, who was rather silly and slightly deaf.

The King bent first over Oliver and then over Grace Fullwobble and sniffed deeply. 'Relish-worthymost raspberry,' he crooned. 'Gorgeous-fullest gooseberry.'

'When will you eat them, Your Majesty?' asked the fat sergeant-major, who was sometimes left the scrapes (if the King was in a good temper and did not give them to the jelly hound).

'I shall have them set for tomorrow,' said the King. 'For pudding after the jelly giraffe.'

'Oh, do eat them tonight, Your Grace,' said the fat sergeant-major.

'Tonight I am eating the jelly elephant at my midnight feast,' said the King. 'One must not make a pig of oneself. It sets a bad example.'

Then they hurried from the room to prepare for the midnight feast, wiping their bright pink, watering mouths.

As soon as they had gone, Bethany opened the window and pressed her head against the bars. They were too narrow to let her in.

'I say,' she said. 'There's another jelly besides Oliver. It's a girl and she's gooseberry.'

'How do you know it's a girl if she's melted?' asked the youngest sister.

'There's a rag doll floating about where her arms should be, of course,' said Bethany.

'We'll never be able to rescue poor Oliver,' said another sister. 'The bars are much too tight.'

'I have an idea,' said Bethany. 'You wait here.'

She hurried to the drinking-straw factory in the village and knocked up the chief drinking-straw man. He was very grumpy at being got out of bed in the middle of the night until Bethany told him what was at stake.

'I'll come at once,' he said, and in his eagerness to help he put his trousers on backwards.

Drinking-straws, of course, are only as long as pencils when you get them in a café, but they are not made like

that. First of all they are made as long as a cricket pitch, and only then are they snipped into pencil lengths. The factory was chock-a-block with drinking-straws standing up with their heads touching the ceiling. Bethany grabbed an armful and ran back to the palace.

She gave a straw to each of her sisters and took one herself. They poked them through the bars and into Oliver's bath and started to suck.

'Don't anybody dare to swallow,' said Bethany. 'Any girl who swallows her brother is a beast.'

The girls emptied each mouthful into a zinc bathtub which Bethany had been wise enough to bring, and soon it was full of Oliver.

Mrs Trimble had Oliver's Waterford crystal mould waiting when they arrived. She gave it a final polish with a new washleather and then emptied Oliver in.

All the family were sitting contentedly around the mould, watching Oliver start to set, when Bethany clapped a hand to her mouth and cried: 'Goodness me!'

'What's the matter?' everybody said, jumping up and thinking of fat sergeant-majors and jelly hounds.

'Grace Fullwobble,' said Bethany. 'We can't leave her there to be the King's pudding.'

So they all trooped off with the zinc bath and the giant drinking-straws to rescue the gooseberry girl.

They had emptied Grace into the bathtub and were tiptoeing from the palace when they heard a terrible laugh. Instead of running away, as I would have done, they crept to the window where the noise had come from. They pressed their noses to the glass and saw an unbelievable sight.

There sat the King, at a mighty oak table, dipping a great golden spoon into – an elephant. Or, rather, half an elephant, for he had already eaten a great deal of it. Only its top part was left – its front legs and shoulders, and its head, which wore a sad and thoughtful look.

Its trunk was too long for the royal jelly bowl and dangled over the edge of the table. The jelly hound, which was chained to a table leg, kept trying to lick the trunk but every time this happened the two fat sergeant-majors kicked its enormous nose with their great boots.

It was this that was making the King laugh.

With every fresh mouthful that the King swallowed the children's eyes grew bigger and their mouths opened wider, for the fearfullest thing was happening. The King was growing bigger and bigger, and rounder and rounder, like a gigantic balloon being inflated with a stirrup pump. Soon his crown looked like a curtain ring on top of a geographical globe. His clothes burst at the seams and fell to the floor. He was sitting there naked, like an ever-growing pink moon, and he was still shovelling jelly down his throat.

The fat sergeant-majors were staring in alarm. One of them put his fingers in his ears and screwed his eyes tight. The other followed suit, and the jelly hound, creeping from under the table to see what was going on, gave a great howl and put its paws in its ears.

Oliver's sisters put their fingers in their ears just in time. Another second and they would have been stone deaf for life. For the King had just spooned up the last morsel of jelly elephant – the final two and a half feet of its trunk – when his skin went terribly tight-looking, and turned blue, and stretched with a horrible creaking sound. And then the King blew to invisible bits with a bang that was heard in Bombay, and a jelly elephant was suddenly trotting up and down the room, looking a little startled but otherwise quite well.

The jelly hound and the fat sergeant-majors were blown to bits, too.

The new King only ate bread and butter and rice pudding, and Oliver Trimble was never in danger again. As soon as the heatwave was over he married Grace Fullwobble, and they had so many jelly babies that they had to send hundreds of them to live in glass jars that you may see in sweet shops. You will never eat one, I hope.

KEN WHITMORE

THE BIRTHDAY PRESENT

One morning a word wizard was walking home from a successful all-night wizards' party given to open the Monster Sale at the Wizards' Bargain Stores. He heard voices coming through an open window. Mr and Mrs Delmonico were having breakfast and discussing important business. The word wizard, who liked to know about other people's business, stopped and listened carefully.

'Our dear twins are growing up,' sighed Mrs Delmonico. 'Sarah is so dashing with her beautiful black curls and shining eyes, and Francis is every bit her equal. He says he wants to be an astronomer and study comets. Do you think that is a good career for a boy?'

'I would rather he went into real estate,' Mr Delmonico replied. 'There is a lot of money in land.'

'And what shall we give the twins for their birthday?' Mrs Delmonico went on. 'What about a pet of some kind? Children love a pet.'

Mr Delmonico did not want his twins, Sarah and Francis, to have pets, but he did not like to argue with his wife. He decided to get his own way by cunning.

'What a good idea!' he exclaimed. 'I wish I could have ideas like yours, my dear. What sort of pet do you have in mind?'

'A pony perhaps,' Mrs Delmonico said doubtfully, but her husband said:

'What a pity! You know I can't stand creatures with eight legs.'

'But, Mr Delmonico, my love, horses don't have eight legs. You're thinking of spiders.'

'Oh!' said Mr Delmonico rather crossly, 'how many legs do they have then?'

'Four each,' Mrs Delmonico told him.

Mr Delmonico smiled. 'But we'd have to get two ponies – one for Sarah and one for Francis. Two horses with four legs each. That makes eight I'm sure you'll agree, my dear.'

'Oh, goodness me, yes, so it does,' sighed Mrs Delmonico.

('This man is a very tricky customer!' thought the word wizard listening carefully.)

'Well then, what about a dog?' asked Mrs Delmonico.

'A dog!' muttered Mr Delmonico pretending to consider. 'The trouble with dogs is their barking.'

'Oh, Mr Delmonico, a dog's bark is harmless.'

'No,' Mr Delmonico replied quickly, 'I understand a dog's bark can be worse than his bite, and not only that – dogs are well known for barking up the wrong tree. I don't think a dog would suit this family. We've got so many trees in the garden the poor dog would wear himself out trying to find the right tree to bark up. No. I don't think a dog would do.'

'Well, what about a kitten?' asked Mrs Delmonico, crunching toast daintily. 'Kittens are pretty and, besides, they're a good investment. Cats have nine lives you know.'

'True! True!' answered Mr Delmonico, supping his hot coffee. 'But they have their disadvantages. You know how any music on the violin brings on my hay fever.'

'But, dear, what does a violin have to do with a kitten for the twins?'

'Don't you remember, "Hey diddle diddle, the cat and the fiddle"?' Mr Delmonico cried.

'But, dear Mr Delmonico, that was only one cat,' his wife protested.

'If one can play the fiddle they all can,' Mr Delmonico declared. 'I don't fancy taking the risk. Besides, they're so everyday and all over the place, cats. How about something more unusual?'

'What do you say to a lion, then?' Mrs Delmonico asked. 'Lions are very beautiful and very brave. There is a well-known saying, "As bold as a lion".'

'Oh, my dear,' Mr Delmonico exclaimed laughing, 'the real saying is, "Bald as a lion". Lions are only beautiful to begin with. On their second birthdays they suddenly go instantaneously bald, and the chairs and the carpets are covered in lion hair.'

Mrs Delmonico supped a cup of tea in a disappointed fashion. 'I should hate that,' she said. 'Perhaps we'd better get the twins a pet next year.'

'Goodness me, what a woman you are for good ideas,' cried Mr Delmonico. 'You are very wise, my dear. Leave the twins' birthday presents to me.'

('Well,' thought the wizard, 'here's a man who uses words for the purposes of confustication. Here's a man who chops words and changes meanings. A word wizard can't stand for that. I'll teach him a lesson. Let me see now – what can I contrive?')

The wizard tossed an idea into the air. It buzzed off like a mosquito, over the lawn straight to Mr Delmonico and stung him on the end of his nose.

Mr Delmonico brought his twins, Sarah and Francis, presents beginning with 'C', like cameras and crayons, clarinets and comics, and a great big fire-engine-red Christmas cracker. It had a black label on it, saying:

'Beware. Monster Cracker.'

'I bought it at the Wizards' Bargain Store Monster

Sale,' Mr Delmonico said. 'I can't wait to see what's inside it.'

Francis took one end and Sarah took the other. They pulled and they pulled and they pulled and they pulled, and then, suddenly, the cracker burst with a snap and a roar like a cannon let off in a cave full of echoes. The room filled with smoke and the smell of gunpowder.

But when the smoke cleared away there, sitting in the middle of the floor, was a monster.

It had eight legs and carried a violin tucked under its chin. It wore a collar and tie and had a hundred teeth, all sharp. It had horns and hairy ears, but the top of its head was quite bald. It smiled at Sarah and Francis and barked.

'A monster! A monster!' cried the twins. 'At last we've got a pet. Thank you, thank you, darling father.'

Mr Delmonico had to let them keep it, of course, but he couldn't help feeling that someone had got the better of him after all.

FROM *NONSTOP NONSENSE*,
MARGARET MAHY

THE LITTLE MOUSE,
THE LITTLE BIRD AND
THE FRIED SAUSAGE

Once upon a time a little mouse, a little bird and a fried sausage decided to live together. For a long time they were very happy and peaceful and they didn't go short of anything.

The little bird's job was to fly into the woods each day to collect firewood. The mouse fetched the water, lit the fire and laid the table. And the fried sausage cooked the meals.

But even those who have everything are never satisfied, and one day the little bird was flying about when he met another bird and told him all about his good life. But the other bird pooh-poohed his story. 'What a poor wretch you are! Just fancy, having to rush about looking for firewood while the other two are just lazing around at home.'

As a matter of fact, when the mouse had lit the fire and fetched the water it did manage to snatch a rest until it was time to lay the table. And the fried sausage just stayed near the oven to make sure the meal was cooking properly and then, when mealtime came, it wriggled like greased lightning through the porridge or the broth and in no time at all the soup was greased, salted and ready.

When the little bird reached home, it put its load of wood down and joined the others at the table. When they had finished their meal, they all went to bed and slept like a log until next day. Altogether, it was a marvellous life!

But because of what the other bird had said, the little bird refused to go into the woods next day. 'I've been your servant long enough,' he said, 'and a real muggins. It's time we tried another way of running the house.'

The mouse and the sausage both pleaded with the bird to keep everything as it was, but it was no good. The bird put his foot down, so they agreed to try a change. They drew lots to see who would do what. The sausage drew the shortest straw, so he had to fetch firewood. The mouse became the cook. And the bird's job was to go for the water.

So what happened then? The sausage went marching off to the woods, the bird lit the fire and the mouse put the saucepan on the oven. And the bird and the mouse waited for a long time for the sausage to come back with the firewood. But he didn't return and soon they started to worry about him.

So the bird flew off to look for him and before long he met a dog on the road. Now, this dog had seen the sausage going to the woods and had decided that he was very easy prey. So he had leapt on him, knocked him down and finished him off.

'But how could you do such a thing?' the bird cried bitterly.

'It's no use crying,' said the dog. 'That sausage was up to no good. I was quite right to do him in.'

There was nothing the bird could do about it, so he picked up his firewood and went home, to tell the mouse what had happened.

They both felt very upset, but decided to make the best of a bad job and carry on as usual. So the bird laid the table and the mouse prepared the meal. Just before he served the broth, the mouse went wriggling through it to put some grease in it, just as the sausage used to do. But before he got to the middle of the saucepan, he drowned.

Then the bird came in to serve the meal. But where was the cook? Nowhere to be seen! So the bird threw the firewood down, shouted for the mouse and looked all over the room, but could find no trace of him.

And then the flames of the fire reached the firewood that the bird had thrown down so carelessly and in no time at all there was a great blaze. The bird went rushing out to the well, to get some water, but the bucket was too heavy and fell down the well, pulling the bird after it. So the bird was drowned.

And that was the end of the little mouse, the little bird and the fried sausage.

THE BROTHERS GRIMM

THE LOVE STORY OF A SPUD

Once upon a time, there was a spud, a plain old spud, the sort you see every day, but this spud was consumed with ambition. She dreamed of becoming a chip. And that is probably exactly what would have happened to her, had the little boy of the house not stolen her from the kitchen.

Once safely in his room with his booty, the little boy took a knife out of his pocket and started to carve the spud. He started by making two eyes. Suddenly the spud could see. Then he made two ears – and the spud could hear! Finally, he made a mouth and the spud could even speak. Then, he made her look in the mirror and said, 'Look how beautiful you are.'

'Oh, horrors!' said the spud. 'I'm nothing of the sort! I look like a human! I was much better before!'

'Oh, all right then,' said the little boy, rather miffed. 'If that's how you feel about it . . .' And he threw her into the dustbin.

Early next morning, the dustbin was emptied and that same day the spud found herself on a big pile of rubbish in the middle of the countryside.

'What a lovely place,' she said, 'and such a nice class of person. There are masses of interesting people here

'. . . Oh, look! Who is this lady who looks like a frying pan?'

(In fact, it was an old guitar almost split in half with only two strings left.)

'Good-day, Madam,' said the spud. 'From what I can see, you must be a most distinguished person, for you look exactly like a frying pan.'

'How kind of you,' said the guitar. 'I don't know what a frying pan is, but thank you all the same. You're quite right, I'm not just anyone. I'm called guitar. And you?'

'Well, I'm called potato. But you can call me spud, because as of today I consider you to be a very dear friend. And as you are a dear friend, I will tell you that on account of my beauty, I had been chosen to become a chip. And I would be one now, had I not had the misfortune to be stolen from the kitchen by the little boy of the house. Of course, after having stolen me, the little beast completely disfigured me by giving me two eyes, two ears and a mouth . . .' And the spud started to snivel.

'Come on. Don't cry,' said the guitar. 'You're still very pretty. And anyway, now you can speak . . .'

'That's true,' agreed the spud. 'It's a great consolation. Well, to finish my story, when I saw what the little monster had done to me, I got angry, took his knife from him, cut off his nose and ran away.' (This, of course, was not true, but the guitar didn't know any better.)

'Quite right too,' said the guitar.

'Yes, I thought so,' agreed the spud. 'But tell me, what about you, how did you get here?'

'Well,' said the guitar, 'for many years, I was the best friend of a young and handsome boy who loved me tenderly. He would bend over me, take me in his arms, stroke me, tap me, strum my tummy and sing me such beautiful songs . . .' The guitar sighed, then her voice became bitter and she continued, 'One day, he came home with a stranger. She was a guitar too, but made of metal, heavy and vulgar and so stupid! She took my friend away from me, she bewitched him. I'm sure she didn't love him. When he took her, it wasn't to sing tender songs to her, oh no! He strummed her furiously, screaming like a wild thing, rolling around on the floor with her. You would have thought they were fighting!

And anyway, he didn't trust her. The proof of that is that he kept her on a leash.'

(In fact, the young and handsome boy had bought an electric guitar and what the guitar took to be a leash was in fact the lead which connected it to the plug.)

'Anyway, the fact of the matter is that she stole him away from me. After a few days, he had eyes only for her, he didn't give me a second glance. And when I saw that, well, I felt that I simply had to go.'

(The guitar was lying. She hadn't gone of her own accord, her master had thrown her out. But she would never have admitted it.

The spud, however, didn't know any better.)

'How beautiful, how touching!' the spud cried. 'Your story has moved me deeply. I know we were made to understand one another. And do you know, the more I look at you, the more I think you look like a frying pan.'

While they were chatting, a tramp who was walking along the road heard them, and stopped to listen.

'You don't see that every day,' he thought. 'An old guitar telling her life story to an old spud, and the spud answering! If I play my cards right, my fortune is made!'

He took the spud, put her in his pocket, then grabbed the guitar and went off to the next town.

In this town, there was a large square and on this square there was a circus. The tramp went and knocked at the manager's door.

'Mr Manager, Mr Manager.'

'Come in. What do you want?'

The tramp climbed into the caravan.

'Mr Manager, I've got a talking guitar!'

'What? A talking guitar?'

'Yes, yes, Mr Manager, sir, and a spud that answers!'

'*What?* What's all this about? Are you drunk, my good man?'

'No, no! I'm not drunk! Just listen!'

The tramp put the guitar on the table, then he took the spud out of his pocket and put it next to her.

'Go on, then. Talk, the two of you!'

Silence.

'Come on, then. You must have something to say to each other.'

Silence.

'Speak, I tell you!'

Still not a word. The manager became very red.

'Look here, my good man, have you come here to make me look a fool?'

'Oh no, Mr Manager, sir! Honest, guv, they can both talk! They're just sulking at the moment, on purpose to annoy me.'

'Get out!'

'But when they're all alone –'

'Get out, I say!'

'But, Mr Manager, sir –'

'What! Are you still here? Right, I'm going to kick you out myself!'

The manager grabbed the tramp by the seat of his trousers and *Whoosh*! threw him out. But, at that moment, he heard a great peal of laughter behind him. It was the spud, no longer able to control herself, who was saying to the guitar, 'Well, we got him there, didn't we? Heeheehee!'

'I'll say we did!' answered the guitar. 'Hahaha!'

The manager turned round.

'So, it was true! You can both speak!'

Silence.

'Come on,' continued the manager. 'There's no need to be silent now. It's pointless: I've heard you.'

Silence.

'Pity,' said the manager slyly. 'I had a rather splendid proposition to put to you. An artistic one!'

'Artistic?' said the guitar.

'Do shut up!' whispered the spud.

'But I'm interested in Art, I am!'

'At last,' said the manager, 'I see you're being reasonable. Well, yes, you're both going to work. You're going to become stars.'

'I'd rather be a chip,' objected the spud.

'You, a chip? With your talent? It would be a crime! You'd rather be eaten than become a star?'

'Why should I be eaten? Do chips get eaten?'

'Of course they do! What do you think people make them for?'

'Oh, I didn't know,' said the spud. 'Well, if that's how it is, I agree, I'd rather become a star.'

A week later, all over town, on big yellow posters, one could read the following:

GRAND THINGUMMY WHATSIT CIRCUS
See the clowns! The acrobats!
The circus riders! The tightrope walkers!
The tigers! The horses! The elephants!
The fleas!
And the World Première of
Naomi, the learned spud,
and Agatha, the guitar who plays on her own!

At the first night, there were lots of people, because no one in the area had ever seen anything like it.

When it was their turn to go into the ring, the spud and the guitar walked on gamely, while the orchestra struck up a military march. To begin with, the spud introduced the act. Then the guitar played a difficult piece on her own. Then the spud sang, accompanied by the guitar singing harmony and playing herself. Then the spud pretended to sing out of key and the guitar pretended to correct her. The spud pretended to get cross and both of them pretended to quarrel, to the great delight of the audience. Finally, they pretended to make it up and they sang the last piece as a duet.

It was an enormous success. The act was recorded for radio and television, so the whole world talked about it. The Sultan of Wonkybonk, who saw the act on the news, flew off the very same day in his private aeroplane and went to see the circus manager.

'Good morning, Mr Manager.'

'Good morning, Your Highness. What can I do for you?'

'I want to marry the spud.'

'The spud? But she isn't a human being!'

'Well, I'll buy her, then.'

'But she isn't a thing either . . . She talks, she sings –'

'I'll kidnap her, then!'

'But you have no right!'

'I have every right, because I'm very rich!'

The manager understood that cunning was called for.

'You're making me very unhappy,' he said, snivelling. 'I love that spud. I've become very attached to her.'

'I quite understand,' said the Sultan with slight irony. 'So, I'll buy her from you for a truckload of diamonds!'

'Only one?' asked the manager.

'Two if you want!'

The manager wiped away a tear, blew his nose loudly and added in a trembling voice, 'I think that if you were to go up to three . . .'

'Fine, three and we'll say no more about it!'

The next day, the Sultan left for his sultanate, taking with him the spud and also the guitar, for the two old friends could not bear to be parted. That week, an important newspaper published photographs of the new couple with this headline:

WE LOVE EACH OTHER

In the following weeks, the same weekly published other photographs with slightly different headings. They were successively:

SPUD WEDDING: GOVERNMENT TO STEP IN?

HIDDEN HEARTBREAK OF SPUD WEDDING

TEARFUL SPUD CONFESSES: I CAN'T GO ON!

GUITAR VOWS: I'M LEAVING!

AND YET THEY LOVE EACH OTHER!

LOVE CONQUERS ALL!

With this last headline they published photographs of the wedding. A week later, the papers were talking about something else and now everyone has forgotten all about it.

FROM *CONTES DE LA RUE BROCA*,
PIERRE GRIPARI

THE BELLE OF VALLEJO

Vallejo, California, possesses a young lady of extraordinary beauty. She is, moreover, as intelligent and bold as she is beautiful, and in grappling with a sudden emergency she is probably unequaled by any one of her sex. Naturally, she is the admiration of every young man in the town. In fact, she is beyond the reach of rivalry. The other young ladies of Vallejo are perfectly well aware that it is hopeless for them to enter the lists with her. They never expect to receive calls from marriageable young men except on the off nights of the Vallejo belle, and though they doubtless murmur secretly against this dispensation, they apparently accept it as a law of nature.

For two years the beauty in question, whom we will call Miss Ecks, received the homage of her multitudinous admirers, and took an evident delight in adding to their number. So far from selecting any particular young man for front-gate or back-piazza duty, she preferred to entertain one or two dozen simultaneous admirers in the full blaze of the brilliantly lighted front parlor. It is only fair to add that she was an earnest young woman, who despised coquetry and never dreamed of showing favor to one young man in order to exasperate the rest.

That so brilliant a girl should have finally selected a

meek young minister on whom to lavish her affections was certainly a surprise to all who knew her, and when it was first rumored that she had made such a selection, Vallejo refused to believe it. The minister made his regular nightly calls upon the object of his affections, but an average quantity of eleven other young men never failed to be present. Of course, he could not obtain a single moment of private happiness with his eleven rivals sitting all around the room, unless he made his evening call at a preposterously early hour. He did try this expedient once or twice, but the only result was that the eleven admirers at once followed his example. In these circumstances he began to grow thin with suppressed affection, and the young lady, alarmed at his condition, made up her mind that something must be done without delay.

About three weeks ago the young minister presented himself in his beloved's front parlor at 6.50 p.m., and, in the ten minutes that elapsed before the first of his rivals rang the bell, he painted the misery of courting by battalions in the most harrowing terms. Miss Ecks listened to him with deep sympathy, and promised him that if he would stay until nine o'clock, the last of the objectionable young men would be so thoroughly disposed of that for the rest of the evening he would have the field to himself. Full of confidence in the determination and resources of his betrothed, his spirits returned, and he was about to express his gratitude with his lips, as well as his heart, when the first young man was ushered into the room.

Miss Ecks received her unwelcome guest with great cordiality, and invited him to sit on a chair the back of which was placed close to a door. The door in question opened outward, and upon the top of a flight of stairs leading to the cellar. The latch was old and out of order, and the least pressure would cause it to fly open. In pursuance of a deep-laid plan, Miss Ecks so molded her conversation as to place the visitor at his ease. In a very few moments, he ceased to twist his fingers and writhe his legs, and presently tilted back his chair after the manner of a contented and happy man. No sooner did the back of the chair touch the door than the latter flew open, and the unhappy guest disappeared into the cellar

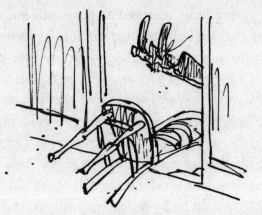

with a tremendous crash. Checking the cry that arose from the astonished clergyman, Miss Ecks quietly reclosed the fatal door, placed a fresh chair in its vicinity, and calmly remarked, 'That's one of them.'

In five minutes more the second young man entered. Like his predecessor, he seated himself on the appointed chair, tipped back upon its hind-legs, and instantly vanished. 'That's two of them,' remarked the imperturbable beauty, as she closed the door and once more re-set the trap. From this time until nine o'clock a constant succession of young men went down those cellar stairs. Some of them groaned slightly after reaching the bottom, but not one returned. It was an unusually good night for young men, and Miss Ecks caught no less than fourteen between seven and nine o'clock. As the last one disappeared she turned to her horrified clergyman and said, 'That's the last of them! Now for business!' but that mild young man had fainted. His nerves were unable to bear the strain, and when the moment of his wished-for monopoly of his betrothed had arrived he was unable to enjoy it.

Later in the evening he revived sufficiently to seek a railway station and fly for ever from his remorseless charmer. The inquest that was subsequently held upon the fourteen young men will long be remembered as a most impressive scene. Miss Ecks was present with her back hair loose, and the tears stood in her magnificent eyes as she testified that she could not imagine what induced the young men to go down the cellar. The jury

without the slightest hesitation found that they had one and all committed suicide, and the coroner personally thanked the young lady for her lucid testimony. She is now more popular than ever, and, with the loss of her own accepted lover, has renewed her former fondness for society, and nightly entertains all the surviving young men of Vallejo.

This shows what the magnificent climate of California can accomplish in the production of girls, when it really tries.

W. L. ALDEN

GERTRUDE THE GOVERNESS: OR,
SIMPLE SEVENTEEN

Synopsis of Previous Chapters: There are no Previous Chapters.

It was a wild and stormy night on the West Coast of Scotland. This, however, is immaterial to the present story, as the scene is not laid in the West of Scotland. For the matter of that the weather was just as bad on the East Coast of Ireland.

But the scene of this narrative is laid in the South of England and takes place in and around Knotacentinum Towers (pronounced as if written Nosham Taws), the seat of Lord Knotacent (pronounced as if written Nosh).

But it is not necessary to pronounce either of these names in reading them.

Nosham Taws was a typical English home. The main part of the house was an Elizabethan structure of warm red brick, while the elder portion, of which the Earl was inordinately proud, still showed the outlines of a Norman Keep, to which had been added a Lancastrian Jail and a Plantagenet Orphan Asylum. From the house in all directions stretched magnificent woodland and park with oaks and elms of immemorial antiquity, while nearer the house stood raspberry bushes and geranium plants which had been set out by the Crusaders.

About the grand old mansion the air was loud with the chirping of thrushes, the cawing of partridges and the clear sweet note of the rook, while deer, antelope and other quadrupeds strutted about the lawn so tame as to eat off the sun-dial. In fact, the place was a regular menagerie.

From the house downwards through the park stretched a beautiful broad avenue laid out by Henry VII.

Lord Nosh stood upon the hearthrug of the library. Trained diplomat and statesman as he was, his stern aristocratic face was upside down with fury.

'Boy,' he said, 'you shall marry this girl or I disinherit you. You are no son of mine.'

Young Lord Ronald, erect before him, flung back a glance as defiant as his own.

'I defy you,' he said. 'Henceforth you are no father of mine. I will get another. I will marry none but a woman I can love. This girl that we have never seen –'

'Fool,' said the Earl, 'would you throw aside our estate and name of a thousand years? The girl, I am told, is beautiful; her aunt is willing; they are French; pah! they understand such things in France.'

'But your reason –'

'I give no reason,' said the Earl. 'Listen, Ronald, I give one month. For that time you remain here. If at the end of it you refuse me, I cut you off with a shilling.'

Lord Ronald said nothing; he flung himself from the room, flung himself upon his horse and rode madly off in all directions.

As the door of the library closed upon Ronald the Earl sank into a chair. His face changed. It was no longer that of the haughty nobleman, but of the hunted criminal. 'He must marry the girl,' he muttered. 'Soon she will know all. Tutchemoff has escaped from Siberia. He knows and will tell. The whole of the mines pass to her, this property with it, and I – but enough.' He rose, walked to the sideboard, drained a dipper full of gin and bitters, and became again a high-bred English gentleman.

It was at this moment that a high dogcart, driven by a groom in the livery of Earl Nosh, might have been seen entering the avenue of Nosham Taws. Beside him sat a young girl, scarce more than a child, in fact not nearly so big as the groom.

The apple-pie hat which she wore, surmounted with black willow plumes, concealed from view a face so face-like in its appearance as to be positively facial.

It was – need we say it – Gertrude the Governess, who was this day to enter upon her duties at Nosham Taws.

At the same time that the dogcart entered the avenue at one end there might have been seen riding down it from the other a tall young man, whose long, aristocratic face proclaimed his birth and who was mounted upon a horse with a face even longer than his own.

And who is this tall young man who draws nearer to Gertrude with every revolution of the horse? Ah, who, indeed? Ah, who, who? I wonder if any of my readers could guess that this was none other than Lord Ronald.

The two were destined to meet. Nearer and nearer they came. And then still nearer. Then for one brief moment they met. As they passed Gertrude raised her head and directed towards the young nobleman two eyes so eye-like in their expression as to be absolutely circular, while Lord Ronald directed towards the occupant of the dogcart a gaze so gaze-like that nothing but a gazelle, or a gas-pipe, could have emulated its intensity.

Was this the dawn of love? Wait and see. Do not spoil the story.

Let us speak of Gertrude. Gertrude DeMongmorenci McFiggin had known neither father nor mother. They had both died years before she was born. Of her mother she knew nothing, save that she was French, was extremely beautiful, and that all her ancestors and even her business acquaintances had perished in the Revolution.

Yet Gertrude cherished the memory of her parents. On her breast the girl wore a locket in which was enshrined a miniature of her mother, while down her neck inside at the back hung a daguerreotype of her father. She carried a portrait of her grandmother up her sleeve and had pictures of her cousins tucked inside her boot, while beneath her – but enough, quite enough.

Of her father Gertrude knew even less. That he was a high-born English gentleman who had lived as a wanderer in many lands, this was all she knew. His only legacy to Gertrude had been a Russian grammar, a Roumanian phrase-book, a theodolite, and a work on mining engineering.

From her earliest infancy Gertrude had been brought up by her aunt. Her aunt had carefully instructed her in Christian principles. She had also taught her Mohammedanism to make sure.

When Gertrude was seventeen her aunt had died of hydrophobia.

The circumstances were mysterious. There had called upon her that day a strange bearded man in the costume of the Russians. After he had left, Gertrude had found her aunt in a syncope from which she passed into an apostrophe and never recovered.

To avoid scandal it was called hydrophobia. Gertrude was thus thrown upon the world. What to do? That was the problem that confronted her.

It was while musing one day upon her fate that Gertrude's eye was struck with an advertisement.

'Wanted a governess; must possess a knowledge of French, Italian, Russian, and Roumanian, Music, and Mining Engineering. Salary £1,4 shillings and 4 pence halfpenny per annum. Apply between half-past eleven and twenty-five minutes to twelve at No. 41 A Decimal

Six, Belgravia Terrace. The Countess of Nosh.'

Gertrude was a girl of great natural quickness of apprehension, and she had not pondered over this announcement more than half an hour before she was struck with the extraordinary coincidence between the list of items desired and the things that she herself knew.

She duly presented herself at Belgravia Terrace before the Countess, who advanced to meet her with a charm which at once placed the girl at her ease.

'You are proficient in French?' she asked.

'*Oh, oui,*' said Gertrude modestly.

'And Italian?' continued the Countess.

'*Oh, si,*' said Gertrude.

'And German?' said the Countess in delight.

'*Ah, ja,*' said Gertrude.

'And Russian?'

'*Yaw.*'

'And Roumanian?'

'*Jep.*'

Amazed at the girl's extraordinary proficiency in modern languages, the Countess looked at her narrowly. Where had she seen those lineaments before? She passed her hand over her brow in thought, and spit upon the floor, but no, the face baffled her.

'Enough,' she said, 'I engage you on the spot; to-morrow you go down to Nosham Taws and begin teaching the children. I must add that in addition you will be expected to aid the Earl with his Russian correspondence. He has large mining interests at Tschminsk.'

Tschminsk! why did the simple word reverberate upon Gertrude's ears? Why? Because it was the name written in her father's hand on the title page of his book on mining. What mystery was here?

It was on the following day that Gertrude had driven up the avenue.

She descended from the dogcart, passed through a phalanx of liveried servants drawn up seven-deep, to each of whom she gave a sovereign as she passed and entered Nosham Taws.

'Welcome,' said the Countess, as she aided Gertrude to carry her trunk upstairs.

The girl presently descended and was ushered into the library, where she was presented to the Earl. As soon as the Earl's eye fell upon the face of the new governess he started visibly. Where had he seen those lineaments? Where was it? At the races, or the theatre – on a bus – no. Some subtler thread of memory was stirring in his mind. He strode hastily to the sideboard, drained a dipper and a half of brandy, and became again the perfect English gentleman.

While Gertrude has gone to the nursery to make the acquaintance of the two tiny golden-haired children who are to be her charges, let us say something here of the Earl and his son.

Lord Nosh was the perfect type of the English nobleman and statesman. The years that he had spent in the diplomatic service at Constantinople, St Petersburg, and Salt Lake City had given to him a peculiar finesse and noblesse, while his long residence at St Helena, Pitcairn Island, and Hamilton, Ontario, had rendered him impervious to external impressions. As deputy-paymaster of the militia of the county he had seen something of the sterner side of military life, while his hereditary office of Groom of the Sunday Breeches had brought him into direct contact with Royalty itself.

His passion for outdoor sports endeared him to his tenants. A keen sportsman, he excelled in fox-hunting, dog-hunting, pig-killing, bat-catching and the pastimes of his class.

In this latter respect Lord Ronald took after his father. From the start the lad had shown the greatest promise. At Eton he had made a splendid showing at battledore and shuttlecock, and at Cambridge had been first in his class at needlework. Already his name was whispered in connection with the All England ping-pong champion-ship, a triumph which would undoubtedly carry with it a seat in Parliament.

Thus was Gertrude the Governess installed at Nosham Taws.

The days and the weeks sped past.

The simple charm of the beautiful orphan girl attracted all hearts. Her two little pupils became her slaves. 'Me loves oo,' little Rasehellfrida would say, leaning her golden head in Gertrude's lap. Even the servants loved her. The head gardener would bring a bouquet of beauti-ful roses to her room before she was up, the second gardener a bunch of early cauliflowers, the third a spray

of late asparagus, and even the tenth and eleventh a sprig of mangel-wurzel or an armful of hay. Her room was full of gardeners all the time, while at evening the aged butler, touched at the friendless girl's loneliness, would tap softly at her door to bring her a rye whisky and seltzer or a box of Pittsburg Stogies. Even the dumb creatures seemed to admire her in their own dumb way. The dumb rooks settled on her shoulder and every dumb dog around the place followed her.

And Ronald! ah, Ronald! Yes, indeed! They had met. They had spoken.

'What a dull morning,' Gertrude had said. '*Quel triste matin! Was fur ein allerverdamnter Tag!*'

'Beastly,' Ronald had answered.

'Beastly!!' The word rang in Gertrude's ears all day.

After that they were constantly together. They played tennis and ping-pong in the day, and in the evening, in accordance with the stiff routine of the place, they sat down with the Earl and Countess to twenty-five-cent poker, and later still they sat together on the verandah and watched the moon sweeping in great circles around the horizon.

It was not long before Gertrude realized that Lord Ronald felt towards her a warmer feeling than that of mere ping-pong. At times in her presence he would fall, especially after dinner, into a fit of profound subtraction.

Once at night, when Gertrude withdrew to her chamber and before seeking her pillow, prepared to retire as a preliminary to disrobing – in other words, before going to bed, she flung wide the casement (opened the window) and perceived (saw) the face of Lord Ronald. He was sitting on a thorn bush beneath her, and his upturned face wore an expression of agonized pallor.

Meantime the days passed. Life at the Taws moved in the ordinary routine of a great English household. At 7 a gong sounded for rising, at 8 a horn blew for breakfast, at 8.30 a whistle sounded for prayers, at 1 a flag was run up at half-mast for lunch, at 4 a gun was fired for afternoon tea, at 9 a first bell sounded for dressing, at 9.15 a second bell for going on dressing, while at 9.30 a rocket was sent up to indicate that dinner was ready. At midnight dinner was over, and at 1 a.m. the tolling of a bell summoned the domestics to evening prayers.

Meanwhile the month allotted by the Earl to Lord Ronald was passing away. It was already July 15, then within a day or two it was July 17, and, almost immediately afterwards, July 18.

At times the Earl, in passing Ronald in the hall, would say sternly, 'Remember, boy, your consent, or I disinherit you.'

And what were the Earl's thoughts of Gertrude? Here was the one drop of bitterness in the girl's cup of happiness. For some reason that she could not divine the Earl showed signs of marked antipathy.

Once as she passed the door of the library he threw a bootjack at her. On another occasion at lunch alone with her he struck her savagely across the face with a sausage.

It was her duty to translate to the Earl his Russian correspondence. She sought in it in vain for the mystery. One day a Russian telegram was handed to the Earl. Gertrude translated it to him aloud.

'Tutchemoff went to the woman. She is dead.'

On hearing this the Earl became livid with fury, in fact this was the day that he struck her with the sausage.

Then one day while the Earl was absent on a bat hunt, Gertrude, who was turning over his correspondence, with that sweet feminine instinct of interest that rose superior to ill-treatment, suddenly found the key to the mystery.

Lord Nosh was not the rightful owner of the Taws. His distant cousin of the older line, the true heir, had died in a Russian prison to which the machinations of the Earl, while Ambassador at Tschminsk, had consigned him. The daughter of this cousin was the true owner of Nosham Taws.

The family story, save only that the documents before her withheld the name of the rightful heir, lay bare to Gertrude's eye.

Strange is the heart of woman. Did Gertrude turn from the Earl with spurning? No. Her own sad fate had taught her sympathy.

Yet still the mystery remained! Why did the Earl start perceptibly each time that he looked into her face? Sometimes he started as much as four centimetres, so that one could distinctly see him do it. On such occasions he would hastily drain a dipper of rum and vichy water and become again the correct English gentleman.

The denouement came swiftly. Gertrude never forgot it.

It was the night of the great ball at Nosham Taws. The whole neighbourhood was invited. How Gertrude's heart had beat with anticipation, and with what trepidation she had overhauled her scant wardrobe in order to appear not unworthy in Lord Ronald's eyes. Her resources were poor indeed, yet the inborn genius for dress that she inherited from her French mother stood her in good stead. She twined a single rose in her hair and contrived herself a dress out of a few old newspapers and the inside of an umbrella that would have graced a court. Round her waist she bound a single braid of bagstring, while a piece of old lace that had been her mother's was suspended to her ear by a thread.

Gertrude was the cynosure of all eyes. Floating to the

strains of the music she presented a picture of bright
girlish innocence that no one could see undisenraptured.

The ball was at its height. It was away up!

Ronald stood with Gertrude in the shrubbery. They
looked into one another's eyes.

'Gertrude,' he said, 'I love you.'

Simple words, and yet they thrilled every fibre in the
girl's costume.

'Ronald!' she said, and cast herself about his neck.

At this moment the Earl appeared standing beside
them in the moonlight. His stern face was distorted with
indignation.

'So!' he said, turning to Ronald, 'it appears that you have chosen!'

'I have,' said Ronald with hauteur.

'You prefer to marry this penniless girl rather than the heiress I have selected for you.'

Gertrude looked from father to son in amazement.

'Yes,' said Ronald.

'Be it so,' said the Earl, draining a dipper of gin which he carried, and resuming his calm. 'Then I disinherit you. Leave this place, and never return to it.'

'Come, Gertrude,' said Ronald tenderly, 'let us flee together.'

Gertrude stood before them. The rose had fallen from her head. The lace had fallen from her ear and the bag-string had come undone from her waist. Her newspapers were crumpled beyond recognition. But dishevelled and illegible as she was, she was still mistress of herself.

'Never,' she said firmly. 'Ronald, you shall never make this sacrifice for me.' Then to the Earl, in tones of ice, 'There is a pride, sir, as great even as yours. The daughter of Metschnikoff McFiggin need crave a boon from no one.'

With that she hauled from her bosom the daguerreotype of her father and pressed it to her lips.

The Earl started as if shot. 'That name!' he cried, 'that face! that photograph! stop!'

There! There is no need to finish; my readers have long since divined it. Gertrude was the heiress.

The lovers fell into one another's arms. The Earl's proud face relaxed. 'God bless you,' he said. The Countess and the guests came pouring out upon the lawn. The breaking day illuminated a scene of gay congratulations.

Gertrude and Ronald were wed. Their happiness was complete. Need we say more? Yes, only this. The Earl was killed in the hunting-field a few days after. The Countess was struck by lightning. The two children fell down a well. Thus the happiness of Gertrude and Ronald was complete.

FROM *NONSENSE NOVELS*,
STEPHEN LEACOCK

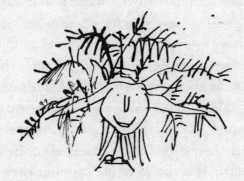

MAGGIE MCWHISTLE

Born in an obscure Scotch manse of Jacobite parents, Maggie McWhistle goes down to immortality as perhaps the greatest heroine of Scottish history; and perhaps not. We read of her austere Gallic beauty in every record and tome of the period – one of the noble women whose paths were lit for them from birth by Destiny's relentless lamp. What did Maggie know of the part she was to play in the history of her country? Nothing. She lived through her girlhood unheeding; she helped her mother with the baps and her father with the haggis; occasionally she would be given a new plaidie – she who might have had baps, haggis, and plaidies ten thousandfold for the asking. A word must be said of her parents. Her father, Jaimie, known all along Deeside as Handsome Jaimie – how the light-hearted village girls mourned when he turned minister: he was high, high above them. Of his meeting with Janey McToddle, the Pride of Bonny Donside, very little is written. Some say that they met in a snowstorm on Ben Lomond, where she was tending her kine; others say that they met on the high road to Aberdeen and his collie Jeannie bit her collie Jock – thus cementing a friendship that was later on to ripen into more and more – and even Maggie. Some years later they were wed, and Jaimie led his girl-bride to the little manse which was destined to be the birthplace of one of Scotland's saviours. History tells us little of Maggie McWhistle's childhood: she apparently lived and breathed like any more ordinary girl – her girdle cakes were famous adown the length and breadth of Aberdeen. Gradually a little path came to be worn between the manse and the kirk, seven miles away, where Maggie's feet so often trod their way to their devotions. She was intensely religious.

One day a stranger came to Aberdeen. He had braw, braw red knees and bonnie, bonnie red hair. History tells us that on first seeing Maggie in her plaidie he smiled, and that the second time he saw her he guffawed, so light-hearted was he.

One day he called at the manse, chucked Maggie under the chin, and ate one of her baps. Eight years later he came again, and, after tweaking her nose, ate a little haggis. By then something seemed to have told her that he was her hero.

One dark night, so the story runs, there came a hammering on the door. Maggie leapt out of her truckle, and wrapping her plaidie round her, for she was a modest girl, she ran to the window.

'Wha is there?' she cried in Scotch.

The answer came back through the darkness, thrilling her to the marrow:

'Bonnie Prince Charlie!'

Maggie gave a cry, and, running downstairs, opened the door and let him in. She looked at him in the light shed by her homely candle. His brow was amuck with sweat: he was trembling in every limb; his ears were scarlet.

'What has happened?'

'I am pursued,' he replied, hoarse with exertion and weariness. 'Hide me, bonnie lassie, hide me, hide me!'

Quick as thought, Maggie hid him behind the door, and not a moment too soon. Then she displayed that strength of will and courage which were to stamp her as a heroine for all time. There came a fresh hammering on the door. Maggie opened it defiantly, and never flinched at the sight of so many brawny men; she only wrapped her plaidie more tightly round her.

'We want Bonnie Prince Charlie,' said the leader, in Scotch.

Then came Maggie's well-known answer, also in Scotch:

'Know you not that this is a manse?'

History has it that the man fell back as though struck, and one by one, awed by the still purity of the white-faced girl, the legions departed into the night whence they had come. Thus Maggie McWhistle proved herself the saviour of Bonnie Prince Charlie for the first time.

There were many occasions after that in which she

was able to prove herself a heroine for his sake. She would conceal him up the chimney or in the oven at the slightest provocation. Soon there were no trees for thirty miles round in which she had not hidden him at some period or another.

Poor Maggie – perchance she is finding in heaven the peaceful rest which was so lacking in her life on earth. For legend hath it that she never had two consecutive nights' sleep for fifteen years, so busy was she saving Bonnie Prince Charlie.

Then came that great deed which even now finds an exultant echo in the heart of every true Scotsman – that deed which none but a bonnie, hardy Highland lassie could have got away with . . . You all know of the massing of James's troops at Carlisle, and later at Glasgow, and later still at Aberdeen. Poor Prince Charlie – so sonsie and braw, a fugitive in his own land – he fled to Loch Morich, followed by Maggie McWhistle in her plaidie, carrying some haggis and baps to comfort him in his exile. History is rather hazy as to exactly what happened; but anyhow, Maggie, with the tattered banner of her country fast unfurling in her heart, decided to save her hero for the last time; and it was well she did not tarry longer, for he was sore pressed. History relates that two tears fell from his eyes on to the shore. Then Maggie, with a brave smile, handed him a bap.

'Eat,' she said in Scotch; 'you are probably very hungry.'

These simple words, spoken straight from her heart, had the effect, so chroniclers inform us, of pulling him together a bit.

'Where can I hide?' he asked.

Maggie looked at him fearlessly for a moment.

'You shall hide in a tree,' she cried, with sudden inspiration.

Bonnie Prince Charlie fell on his braw red knees.

'Please,' he cried pleadingly, 'could it be an elm? I'm so tired of gnarled oaks.'

'Yes!' cried the courageous girl exultantly. 'Quick, we will trick them yet.'

Then came the supreme moment – the act of sheer devotion that was to brand that simple soul through the ages as a noble martyr in, alas! a lost cause. Shading her

eyes with her hand, she perceived a legion of the enemy
encamped on the one island of which the lonely Gallic
loch boasted. Her woman's wit had devised a plan. Fling-
ing baps and haggis to the winds, she leapt into a boat
and began to row – you all know the story of that fateful
row. Round and round the island she went for three
weeks, never heeding her tired arms and weary hands;
blisters came and went, but she felt them not; her hat
flew off, but the lion-hearted woman never stopped; and
all to convince the troops on the island that it was a
fleet approaching under the command of Bonnie Prince
Charlie. Completely routed, every officer and man swam
to the mainland and beat a retreat, and not until the last
of them had gone did Maggie relinquish her hold on the
creaking oars.

Thus did the strategy of a simple Highland lassie defeat the aims of generals whose hearts and souls had been steeped from birth in the sanguinary ways of war. Of her journey home with the Prince you all know; and what her white-haired father said when she arrived you've heard hundreds of times. There has been a lot of argument as to the exact form the Prince's gratitude took. Some say he unwrapped her plaidie and went away with it; others write that he cut a lock of his braw red hair and gave it to her with his usual merry smile; but the authentic version of that moving scene is that of the burnt scone. Maggie had baked a scone and handed it to him; then, after he had bitten it, he handed it back.

'Nay, lassie, nay,' he is said to have remarked. 'My purse is empty but my heart is full. Take this scone imprinted by my royal teeth, and treasure it.'

Then with a debonair bow and a ready laugh, a mocking shout and a whimsical wink, he went out into dreary Galway – a homeless wanderer.

Of Maggie's death very little is known. Some say she died of hay-fever; others say it was nasal catarrh; but only her old mother, with a woman's unerring instinct, guessed the truth: in reality she died of a broken heart and a burnt scone.

FROM *A WITHERED NOSEGAY*,
NOËL COWARD

THE BEAUTIFULL CASSANDRA

A NOVEL IN TWELVE CHAPTERS

dedicated by permission to Miss Austen.

Dedication.

MADAM

You are a Phoenix. Your taste is refined, your Sentiments are noble, & your Virtues innumerable. Your Person is lovely, your Figure, elegant, & your Form, majestic. Your Manners are polished, your Conversation is rational & your appearance singular. If therefore the following Tale will afford one moment's amusement to you, every wish will be gratified of

> Your most obedient
> humble servant
> THE AUTHOR

CHAPTER THE FIRST

Cassandra was the Daughter & the only Daughter of a celebrated Milliner in Bond Street. Her father was of noble Birth, being the near relation of the Dutchess of — 's Butler.

CHAPTER THE 2^d

When Cassandra had attained her 16th year, she was lovely & amiable & chancing to fall in love with an elegant Bonnet, her Mother had just compleated bespoke by the Countess of — she placed it on her gentle Head & walked from her Mother's shop to make her Fortune.

CHAPTER THE 3^d

The first person she met, was the Viscount of — a young Man, no less celebrated for his Accomplishments & Virtues, than for his Elegance & Beauty. She curtseyed & walked on.

CHAPTER THE 4th

She then proceeded to a Pastry-cooks where she
devoured six ices, refused to pay for them, knocked down
the Pastry Cook & walked away.

CHAPTER THE 5th

She next ascended a Hackney Coach & ordered it to
Hampstead, where she was no sooner arrived than she
ordered the Coachman to turn round & drive her back
again.

CHAPTER THE 6th

Being returned to the same spot of the same Street she had sate out from, the Coachman demanded his Pay.

CHAPTER THE 7th

She searched her pockets over again & again; but every search was unsuccessfull. No money could she find. The man grew peremptory. She placed her bonnet on his head & ran away.

CHAPTER THE 8th

Thro' many a street she then proceeded & met in none the least Adventure till on turning a Corner of Bloomsbury Square, she met Maria.

CHAPTER THE 9th

Cassandra started & Maria seemed surprised; they trembled, blushed, turned pale & passed each other in a mutual silence.

CHAPTER THE 10th

Cassandra was next accosted by her friend the Widow, who squeezing out her little Head thro' her less window, asked her how she did? Cassandra curtseyed & went on.

CHAPTER THE 11th

A quarter of a mile brought her to her paternal roof in Bond Street from which she had now been absent nearly 7 hours.

CHAPTER THE 12th

She entered it & was pressed to her Mother's bosom by that worthy Woman. Cassandra smiled & whispered to herself 'This is a day well spent.'

JANE AUSTEN

BLAME THE FOG

Dr Strabismus (Whom God Preserve) of Utrecht was a victim of the thick fog the other night. He was due to address the St Agnes Study Circle on the skull of the Peking Man (*Sinanthropus Pekinensis*), but went to the wrong place. He entered a crowded hall, dashed on to the platform, and began: 'When we remember that this remarkable thing is about a million years old –' A menacing roar greeted the words, and he was informed by the chairman that he had interrupted the presentation of a rose-bowl to a lady physical-drill instructor.

FROM *THE BEST OF BEACHCOMBER*,
J. B. MORTON

THE STORY OF THE FOUR LITTLE CHILDREN WHO WENT ROUND THE WORLD

Once upon a time, a long while ago, there were four little people whose names were

VIOLET, SLINGSBY, GUY, and LIONEL; and they all thought they should like to see the world. So they bought a large boat to sail quite round the world by sea, and then they were to come back on the other side by land. The boat was painted blue with green spots, and the sail was yellow with red stripes; and when they set off, they only took a small Cat to steer and look after the boat, besides an elderly Quangle-Wangle, who had to cook the dinner and make the tea; for which purposes they took a large kettle.

For the first ten days they sailed on beautifully, and found plenty to eat, as there were lots of fish, and they had only to take them out of the sea with a long spoon, when the Quangle-Wangle instantly cooked them, and the Pussy-cat was fed with the bones, with which she expressed herself pleased on the whole, so that all the party were very happy.

During the day-time, Violet chiefly occupied herself in putting salt-water into a churn, while her three brothers churned it violently, in the hope that it would turn into butter, which it seldom, if ever, did; and in the evening they all retired into the Tea-kettle, where they all managed to sleep very comfortably, while Pussy and the Quangle-Wangle managed the boat.

After a time they saw some land at a distance; and when they came to it, they found it was an island made of water quite surrounded by earth. Besides that, it was bordered by evanescent isthmusses with a great Gulf-stream running about all over it, so that it was perfectly beautiful, and contained only a single tree, 503 feet high.

When they had landed, they walked about, but found to their great surprise that the island was quite full of veal-cutlets and chocolate-drops, and nothing else. So they all climbed up the single high tree to discover, if possible, if there were any people; but having remained on the top of the tree for a week, and not seeing anybody, they naturally concluded that there were no inhabitants, and accordingly when they came down they loaded the boat with two thousand veal-cutlets and a million of chocolate drops, and these afforded them sustenance for more than a month, during which time they pursued their voyage with the utmost delight and apathy.

After this they came to a shore where there were no less than sixty-five great red parrots with blue tails, sitting on a rail all of a row, and all fast asleep. And I am sorry to say that the Pussy-cat and the Quangle-Wangle crept softly and bit off the tail-feathers of all the sixty-five parrots, for which Violet reproved them both severely.

Notwithstanding which, she proceeded to insert all the feathers, two hundred and sixty in number, in her bonnet, thereby causing it to have a lovely and glittering appearance, highly prepossessing and efficacious.

The next thing that happened to them was in a narrow part of the sea, which was so entirely full of fishes that the boat could go on no further; so they remained there about six weeks, till they had eaten nearly all the fishes, which were Soles, and all ready-cooked and covered with shrimp sauce, so that there was no trouble whatever. And as the few fishes who remained uneaten complained of the cold, as well as of the difficulty they had in getting any sleep on account of the extreme noise made by the Arctic Bears and the Tropical Turnspits which fre- quented the neighbourhood in great numbers, Violet most amiably knitted a small woollen frock for several of the fishes, and Slingsby administered some opium drops to them, through which kindness they became quite warm and slept soundly.

Then they came to a country which was wholly covered with immense Orange-trees of a vast size, and quite full of fruit. So they all landed, taking with them the Tea-kettle, intending to gather some of the Oranges and place them in it. But while they were busy about this, a most dreadfully high wind rose, and blew out most of the Parrot-tail feathers from Violet's bonnet. That, however, was nothing compared with the calamity of the Oranges falling down on their heads by millions and millions, which thumped and bumped and bumped and thumped them all so seriously that they were obliged to run as hard as they could for their lives, besides that the sound of the Oranges rattling on the Tea-kettle was of the most fearful and amazing nature.

Nevertheless they got safely to the boat, although considerably vexed and hurt; and the Quangle-Wangle's right foot was so knocked about that he had to sit with his head in his slipper for at least a week.

This event made them all for a time rather melancholy, and perhaps they might never have become less so, had not Lionel, with a most praiseworthy devotion and perseverance, continued to stand on one leg and whistle to them in a loud and lively manner, which diverted the whole party so extremely, that they gradually recovered their spirits, and agreed that whenever they should reach home they would subscribe towards a testimonial to Lionel, entirely made of Gingerbread and Raspberries, as an earnest token of their sincere and grateful infection.

After sailing on calmly for several more days, they came to another country, where they were much pleased and surprised to see a countless multitude of white Mice with red eyes, all sitting in a great circle, slowly eating Custard Pudding with the most satisfactory and polite demeanour.

And as the four Travellers were rather hungry, being tired of eating nothing but Soles and Oranges for so long a period, they held a council as to the propriety of asking the Mice for some of their Pudding in a humble and affecting manner, by which they could hardly be otherwise than gratified. It was agreed therefore that Guy should go and ask the Mice, which he immediately did; and the result was that they gave a Walnut-shell only half full of Custard diluted with water. Now, this displeased Guy, who said, 'Out of such a lot of Pudding as you have got, I must say you might have spared a somewhat larger quantity!' But no sooner had he finished speaking than all the Mice turned round at once, and sneezed at him in an appalling and vindictive manner (and it is impossible to imagine a more scroobious and unpleasant sound than that caused by the simultaneous sneezing of many millions of angry Mice), so that Guy rushed back to the boat, having first shied his cap into the middle of the Custard Pudding, by which means he completely spoiled the Mice's dinner.

By-and-by the Four Children came to a country where there were no houses, but only an incredibly innumerable number of large bottles without corks, and of a dazzling and sweetly susceptible blue colour. Each of these blue bottles contained a Blue-Bottle-Fly, and all these interesting animals live continually together in the most copious and rural harmony, nor perhaps in many parts of the world is such perfect and abject happiness to be found. Violet, and Slingsby, and Guy, and Lionel, were greatly struck with this singular and instructive settlement, and having previously asked permission of the Blue-Bottle-Flies (which was most courteously granted), the Boat was drawn up to the shore and they proceeded to make tea in front of the Bottles; but as they had no tea-leaves, they merely placed some pebbles in the hot water, and the Quangle-Wangle played some tunes over it on an Accordion, by which of course tea was made directly, and of the very best quality.

The Four Children then entered into conversation with the Blue-Bottle-Flies, who discoursed in a placid and genteel manner, though with a slightly buzzing accent, chiefly owing to the fact that they each held a small clothes-brush between their teeth, which naturally occasioned a fizzy extraneous utterance.

'Why,' said Violet, 'would you kindly inform us, do you reside in bottles? and if in bottles at all, why not rather in green or purple, or indeed in yellow bottles?'

To which questions a very aged Blue-Bottle-Fly answered, 'We found the bottles here all ready to live in, that is to say, our great-great-great-great-great-

grandfathers did, so we occupied them at once. And when the winter comes on, we turn the bottles upside-down, and consequently rarely feel the cold at all, and you know very well that this could not be the case with bottles of any other colour than blue.'

'Of course it could not,' said Slingsby; 'but if we may take the liberty of inquiring, on what do you chiefly subsist?'

'Mainly on Oyster-patties,' said the Blue-Bottle-Fly, 'and, when these are scarce, on Raspberry Vinegar and Russian leather boiled down to a jelly.'

'How delicious!' said Guy.

To which Lionel added, 'Huzz!' and all the Blue-Bottle-Flies said 'Buzz!'

At this time, an elderly Fly said it was the hour for the Evening-song to be sung; and on a signal being given all the Blue-Bottle-Flies began to buzz at once in a sumptuous and sonorous manner, the melodious and mucilaginous sounds echoing all over the waters, and resounding across the tumultuous tops of the transitory Titmice upon the intervening and verdant mountains, with a serene and sickly suavity only known to the truly virtuous. The Moon was shining slobaciously from the star-bespringled sky, while her light irrigated the smooth and shiny sides and wings and backs of the Blue-Bottle-Flies with a peculiar and trivial splendour, while all nature cheerfully responded to the cerulaean and conspicuous circumstances.

In many long-after years, the four little Travellers looked back to that evening as one of the happiest in all their lives, and it was already past midnight, when – the Sail of the Boat having been set up by the Quangle-Wangle, the Tea-kettle and Churn placed in their respective positions, and the Pussy-cat stationed at the Helm – the Children each took a last and affectionate farewell of the Blue-Bottle-Flies, who walked down in a body to the water's edge to see the Travellers embark.

As a token of parting respect and esteem, Violet made a curtsey quite down to the ground, and stuck one of her few remaining Parrot-tail feathers into the back hair of the most pleasing of the Blue-Bottle-Flies, while Slingsby, Guy and Lionel offered them three small boxes, containing respectively, Black Pins, Dried Figs and Epsom Salts: and thus they left that happy shore for ever.

Overcome by their feelings, the Four little Travellers instantly jumped into the Tea-kettle, and fell fast asleep. But all along the shore for many hours there was distinctly heard a sound of severely suppressed sobs, and of a vague multitude of living creatures using their pocket-handkerchiefs in a subdued simultaneous snuffle – lingering sadly along the walloping waves as the boat sailed farther and farther away from the Land of the Happy Blue-Bottle-Flies.

Nothing particular occurred for some days after these events, except that as the Travellers were passing a low tract of sand, they perceived an unusual and gratifying spectacle, namely, a large number of Crabs and Crawfish – perhaps six or seven hundred – sitting by the water-side, and endeavouring to disentangle a vast heap of pale pink worsted, which they moistened at intervals with a fluid composed of Lavender-water and White-wine Negus.

'Can we be of any service to you, O crusty Crabbies?' said the Four Children.

'Thank you kindly,' said the Crabs, consecutively. 'We are trying to make some worsted Mittens, but do not know how.'

On which Violet, who was perfectly acquainted with the art of mitten-making, said to the Crabs, 'Do your claws unscrew, or are they fixtures?'

'They are all made to unscrew,' said the Crabs, and forthwith they deposited a great pile of claws close to the boat, with which Violet uncombed all the pale pink worsted, and then made the loveliest Mittens with it you can imagine. These the Crabs, having resumed and screwed on their claws, placed cheerfully upon their wrists, and walked away rapidly on their hind-legs, warbling songs with a silvery voice and in a minor key.

After this the four little people sailed on again till they came to a vast and wide plain of astonishing dimensions, on which nothing whatever could be discovered at first; but as the Travellers walked onward, there appeared in the extreme and dim distance a single object, which on

a nearer approach, and on an accurately cutaneous inspection, seemed to be somebody in a large white wig sitting on an arm-chair made of Sponge Cakes and Oyster-shells. 'It does not quite look like a human being,' said Violet, doubtfully; nor could they make out what it really was, till the Quangle-Wangle (who had previously been round the world), exclaimed softly in a loud voice, 'It is the Co-operative Cauliflower!'

And so in truth it was, and they soon found that what they had taken for an immense wig was in reality the top of the cauliflower, and that he had no feet at all, being able to walk tolerably well with a fluctuating and graceful movement on a single cabbage stalk, an accomplishment which naturally saved him the expense of stockings and shoes.

Presently, while the whole party from the boat was gazing at him with mingled affection and disgust, he suddenly arose, and in a somewhat plumdomphious manner hurried off towards the setting sun – his steps supported by two superincumbent confidential cucumbers, and a large number of Waterwagtails proceeding in advance of him by three-and-three in a row – till he finally disappeared on the brink of the western sky in a crystal cloud of sudorific sand.

So remarkable a sight of course impressed the Four Children very deeply; and they returned immediately to their boat with a strong sense of undeveloped asthma and a great appetite.

Shortly after this the Travellers were obliged to sail directly below some high overhanging rocks, from the top of one of which, a particularly odious little boy, dressed in rose-coloured knickerbockers, and with a pewter plate upon his head, threw an enormous Pumpkin at the boat, by which it was instantly upset.

But this upsetting was of no consequence, because all the party knew how to swim very well, and in fact they preferred swimming about till after the moon rose, when, the water growing chilly, they sponge-taneously entered

the boat. Meanwhile the Quangle-Wangle threw back
the Pumpkin with immense force, so that it hit the rocks
where the malicious little boy in rose-coloured knickerbockers was sitting, when, being quite full of Lucifer-
matches, the Pumpkin exploded surreptitiously into a
thousand bits, whereon the rocks instantly took fire, and
the odious little boy became unpleasantly hotter and
hotter and hotter, till his knickerbockers were turned
quite green, and his nose was burned off.

Two or three days after this had happened, they came
to another place, where they found nothing at all except
some wide and deep pits full of Mulberry Jam. This is
the property of the tiny Yellow-nosed Apes who abound
in these districts, and who store up the Mulberry Jam
for their food in winter, when they mix it with pellucid

pale periwinkle soup, and serve it out in Wedgwood China bowls, which grow freely all over that part of the country. Only one of the Yellow-nosed Apes was on the spot, and he was fast asleep: yet the Four Travellers and the Quangle-Wangle and Pussy were so terrified by the violence and sanguinary sound of his snoring, that they merely took a small cupful of the Jam, and returned to re-embark in their Boat without delay.

What was their horror on seeing the boat (including the Churn and the Tea-kettle) in the mouth of an enormous Seeze Pyder, an aquatic and ferocious creature truly dreadful to behold, and happily only met within those excessive longitudes. In a moment the beautiful boat was bitten into fifty-five-thousand-million-hundred-billion bits, and it instantly became quite clear that Violet, Slingsby, Guy and Lionel could no longer preliminate their voyage by sea.

The Four Travellers were therefore obliged to resolve on pursuing their wanderings by land, and very fortunately there happened to pass by at that moment an elderly Rhinoceros, on which they seized; and all four mounting on his back, the Quangle-Wangle sitting on his horn and holding on by his ears, and the Pussy-cat swinging at the end of his tail, they set off, having only four small beans and three pounds of mashed potatoes to last through their whole journey.

They were, however, able to catch numbers of the chickens and turkeys, and other birds who incessantly alighted on the head of the Rhinoceros for the purpose of gathering the seeds of the rhododendron plants which grew there, and these creatures they cooked in the most translucent and satisfactory manner, by means of a fire lighted on the end of the Rhinoceros's back. A crowd of Kangaroos and Gigantic Cranes accompanied them, from feelings of curiosity and complacency, so that they were never at a loss for company, and went onward as it were in a sort of profuse and triumphant procession.

Thus, in less than eighteen weeks, they all arrived safely at home, where they were received by their admiring relatives with joy tempered with contempt; and where they finally resolved to carry out the rest of their travelling plans at some more favourable opportunity.

As for the Rhinoceros, in token of their grateful adherence, they had him killed and stuffed directly, and then set him up outside the door of their father's house as a Diaphanous Doorscraper.

EDWARD LEAR

HOW GIMME THE AX FOUND OUT ABOUT THE ZIGZAG RAILROAD AND WHO MADE IT ZIGZAG

One day Gimme the Ax said to himself, 'Today I go to the post office and around, looking around. Maybe I will hear about something happening last night when I was sleeping. Maybe a policeman began laughing and fell in a cistern and came out with a wheelbarrow full of goldfish wearing new jewelry. How do I know? Maybe the man in the moon going down a cellar stairs to get a pitcher of buttermilk for the woman in the moon to drink and stop crying, maybe he fell down the stairs and broke the pitcher and laughed and picked up the broken pieces and said to himself, "One, two, three, four, accidents happen in the best regulated families." How do I know?'

So with his mind full of simple and refreshing thoughts, Gimme the Ax went out into the backyard garden and looked at the different necktie poppies growing early in the summer. Then he picked one of the necktie poppies to wear for a necktie scarf going downtown to the post office and around looking around.

'It is a good speculation to look nice around looking around in a necktie scarf,' said Gimme the Ax. 'It is a necktie with a picture like whiteface pony spots on a

green frog swimming in the moonshine.'

So he went downtown. For the first time he saw the Potato Face Blind Man playing an accordion on the corner next nearest the post office. He asked the Potato Face to tell him why the railroad tracks run zigzag in the Rootabaga Country.

'Long ago,' said the Potato Face Blind Man, 'long before the necktie poppies began growing in the backyard, long before there was a necktie scarf like yours with whiteface pony spots on a green frog swimming in the moonshine, back in the old days when they laid the rails for the railroad they laid the rails straight.

'Then the zizzies came. The zizzy is a bug. He runs zigzag on zigzag legs, eats zigzag with zigzag teeth, and spits zigzag with a zigzag tongue.

'Millions of zizzies came hizzing with little hizzers on their heads and under their legs. They jumped on the rails with their zigzag legs, and spit and twisted with their zigzag teeth and tongues till they twisted the whole railroad and all the rails and tracks into a zigzag railroad with zigzag rails for the trains, the passenger trains and the freight trains, all to run zigzag on.

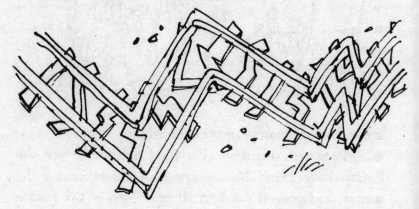

'Then the zizzies crept away into the fields where they sleep and cover themselves with zigzag blankets on special zigzag beds.

'Next day came shovelmen with their shovels, smooth engineers with smooth blue prints, and water boys with water pails and water dippers for the shovelmen to drink after shoveling the railroad straight. And I nearly forgot to say the steam and hoist operating engineers came and began their steam hoist and operating to make the railroad straight.

'They worked hard. They made the railroad straight again. They looked at the job and said to themselves and to each other, "This is it – we done it."

'Next morning the zizzies opened their zigzag eyes and looked over to the railroad and the rails. When they saw the railroad all straight again, and the rails and the ties and the spikes all straight again, the zizzies didn't even eat breakfast that morning.

'They jumped out of their zigzag beds, jumped onto the rails with their zigzag legs and spit and twisted till they spit and twisted all the rails and the ties and the spikes back into a zigzag like the letter Z and the letter Z at the end of the alphabet.

'After that the zizzies went to breakfast. And they said to themselves and to each other, the same as the shovelmen, the smooth engineers and the steam hoist and operating engineers, "This is it – we done it."'

'So that is the how of the which – it was the zizzies,' said Gimme the Ax.

'Yes, it was the zizzies,' said the Potato Face Blind Man. 'That is the story told to me.'

'Who told it to you?'

'*Two little zizzies*. They came to me one cold winter night and slept in my accordion where the music keeps it warm in winter. In the morning I said, "Good morning, zizzies, did you have a good sleep last night and pleasant dreams?" And after they had breakfast they told me the story. Both told it zigzag but it was the same kind of zigzag each had together.'

FROM *ROOTABAGA STORIES*,
CARL SANDBURG

RUNNING DOWN TO THE BEACH

Bottersnikes are the laziest creatures, probably, in the whole world.

They are too lazy to dig burrows, like rabbits, or to find hollow trees to live in as the small animals do, and would be horrified at the work of building nests, like birds. Bottersnikes find their homes readymade, in rubbish heaps. When they find a pile of tins, pots, pans and junk, they think it is lovely, and crawl in. And live there, sleeping mostly. Best of all they like the rubbish heaps along dusty roadsides in the lonely Australian bush, where they can sleep for weeks, undisturbed.

Once, in a rubbish heap like this, two long black ears poked out of a watering can. The ears came first because they were twice as long as the head they belonged to. Between the ears appeared an ugly green face with slanted eyes, a nose like a cheese grater and a mean mouth with pointed teeth sticking out. The skin was wrinkly all over and little toadstools grew where the eyebrows should have been.

This was the King of the Bottersnikes. He squeezed out of the watering can.

The King's ears turned bright red because he was angry – this always happens with Bottersnikes when they get angry – and the cause of his temper was a thistle growing through the bottom of his bed. But he was too lazy to pull it out and just stood there looking, with his ears growing redder. Near him he saw an old rusting car, propped against a gum tree. What a palace that would make for a Bottersnike King! 'If someone would open the door,' he thought, 'I would get in.'

So the King yelled at the top of his voice for help – and very loud that is; but the other Bottersnikes, all twenty or so of the King's band, snored loudly from their beds in the rubbish to show they had not heard.

This meant that the King would have to pull someone out of bed, kick him and twist his tail till he woke up, and make him open the car door, so that the King could get in. Bottersnikes go to no end of trouble to do things

the easiest way. 'There is no one, no one at all,' the King growled, 'who will help.' His ears glowed in a royal rage that was quite terrible to see.

As the King was yelling for help the Gumbles happened to be passing, which was just their bad luck. They were on their way down the hill to a little stream they knew of, called Earlyfruit Creek, where the water flowed into quiet pools and banks of sand made tiny beaches just right for Gumble paddling.

'Hey, you!' bawled the King to the Gumbles. 'Come and open this door and help me in.'

The Gumbles were a bit astonished, as all their friends in the Bush were much politer than this, but being cheerful little creatures and always ready to lend a hand, like good Brownies, they said: 'Well, all right, if it won't take too long, because we're in a hurry to get to the creek, you see.'

'Don't argue,' the King said. 'Just do as you're told.'

By climbing up each other's backs the Gumbles managed to open the car door, and with a one-two-three altogether *shove* they heaved the King into his new palace.

Hearing the strange voices, the other Bottersnikes decided to wake up. They peered at these funny little creatures they'd not seen before and asked: 'What are these?'

'Useful,' the King said, clambering on to the steering wheel, 'that's what they are. Grab 'em.'

'Here, just a minute – you can't do that,' the Gumbles cried, all speaking at once. 'We only stopped to lend a hand. We're just running down to the beach. For a paddle in the cool water.'

'Got you!' shouted the Bottersnikes, and they grabbed those little Gumbles – this was quite easy, for though they are so lazy Bottersnikes can move faster than Gumbles when they have to because their legs are longer. And when they grabbed them they discovered a peculiar thing about Gumbles. They discovered that you can squeeze Gumbles to any shape you like without hurting them, and that if you press them very hard they flatten out like pancakes and cannot pop back to their proper shapes unless helped.

'This,' said the King, watching, 'is more useful than ever.'

The Bottersnikes blinked. They couldn't see why it was useful at all – silly, squashy things, they thought.

'Because,' the King growled, 'we can pop 'em into somethink and squash 'em down hard so's they can't get away, and when I want some more work done they'll be ready and waiting to do it.'

Now the Bottersnikes began to get the idea. They would have servants for ever, to tidy up and keep them comfortable. 'Hoo, hoo!' they yelled. 'What'll we pop 'em into?'

'Jam tins,' roared the King. Another good idea! Naturally there were hundreds of them lying in the rubbish. 'The proper thing is to shout "Got you!" and grab 'em, and pop 'em into jam tins.'

'What a rotten thing to think of,' cried the Gumbles, 'when we only stopped to –'

'Got you!' shouted the Bottersnikes, and they grabbed the Gumbles and popped them into jam tins. And squashed them down hard, with horny fists. There were more than enough Gumbles for each Bottersnike to grab one. Some of the fattest, in fact, grabbed two.

How they snuffled through their noses – which meant that they were laughing – how they rorted and snorted and hooed with glee at what they had done. 'We done ourselves a good turn,' the King announced. 'We done a good day's work.'

Exhausted at the thought of this, they fell asleep at once, and the tinned Gumbles were left in the hot sun all afternoon, thinking of the cool creek where they had meant to paddle. Now, it seemed, they would never go there again.

Towards evening some of the Bottersnikes woke up, disturbed by snores from the King's palace – most royal ones, like trombones blaring. 'All very well for 'im,' the Bottersnikes thought, their ears going red, 'but we ain't got palaces to sleep in, and we ain't comfy, and what's to be done?' Then they remembered the Gumbles. 'Stop being lazy in them tins,' they ordered, 'and come and put our places comfy.'

So the Gumbles were hauled out of the tins and put to work building bigger and better rubbish heaps for the Bottersnikes to crawl into; a nastier job for Gumbles would be impossible to find. 'Harder, harder,' the Bottersnikes bawled, 'and don't try to run away, 'cos we're watching you!'

But they did not see one little Gumble under the King's car, where he was puzzling over a tin-opener he had found. This Gumble was the one who had Tinks – every Tink was a good idea – and as soon as he discovered how the tin-opener worked a real beauty came to him: *Tink*! Clear as if you had tapped the edge of a glass with a spoon.

Up jumped Tinkingumble with his bright idea and peered cautiously from behind a wheel. 'Pssst! Bring me the jam tins one by one,' he whispered to Happigumble and Merrigumble near by. 'Mind they don't see you!'

While the Bottersnikes were trying the new heaps to see if they were comfy, and squabbling over who should have the comfiest, they rolled the jam tins under the car where Tinkingumble cut the bottoms out of every one, working fast and secretly; then Happigumble and Merrigumble rolled them back again taking care to keep the parts together so that they looked all right from the top. The job was done just in time.

'It ain't good,' the Bottersnikes growled, 'not a bit good, but it'll have to do for tonight 'cos we're tired, and you'll have to work harder tomorrow.' They shouted 'Got you!' and grabbed the Gumbles and popped them into the jam tins, and snuffled their noses about it because they knew they'd have servants tomorrow and for ever. Then they went to sleep.

When they were snoring safely Tinkingumble called 'Now!' and the Gumbles tried to stand up. The cut-out bottoms of the tins fell away nicely, just as planned, but they were still stuck in the round parts – absolutely wodged in.

'How are we going to get away?' said Happigumble. 'My legs are so squashed up I can hardly move!'

'I hadn't thought of that,' Tinkingumble said unhappily. A Tink came to the rescue as he spoke – only a small one, but quite clear. Following Tinkingumble's, the jam tins blundered towards the road banging into each other as they went – it nearly made them giggly, and Gumbles are quite hopeless when they go giggly – and there they rocked themselves until the tins fell over on their sides, and the slope of the hill did the rest. The Gumbles ran down to the beach in their jam tins much, much faster than any Bottersnike could have chased them.

An Owl, who saw all the tins rolling down the hill in the moonlight, was so surprised that he flew straight into a moult, and declared he'd never seen such a sight in all his years of hooting.

At the bottom of the hill the Gumbles shot off the road into the Bush, where a friendly bandicoot poked them out of the tins with his long nose. They put the jam tins in a bin marked PLEASE BE TIDY and spent the rest of the night paddling at their favourite beach, for Gumbles are too busy having fun to waste time sleeping and there is no one to tell them when to go to bed.

FROM *BOTTERSNIKES AND GUMBLES*,
S. A. WAKEFIELD

LIVING IN W'ALES

Once there was a man who said he didn't like the sort of houses people lived in, so he built a model village. It was not really like a model village at all, because the houses were all big enough for real people to live in, and he went about telling people to come and Live in W'ales.

There was also living in Liverpool a little girl who was very nice. So when all the people went off with the man to live in W'ales, she went with them. But the man walked so fast that presently some of them got left behind. The ones who were left behind were the little girl, and an Alsatian dog, and a very cross old lady in a bonnet and black beads, who was all stiff, but had a nice husband, who was left behind too.

So they all went along till they came to the sea; and in the sea was a whale. The little girl said, 'That was what he meant, I suppose, about living in W'ales. I expect the others are inside; or, if not, they are in another one.'

So they shouted to know if they might come in, but the whale didn't hear them. The nice husband said that if that was what living in W'ales meant, he would rather go back to Liverpool; but the horrid old lady said, 'Nonsense! I will go and whisper in its ear.'

But she was very silly, and so instead of whispering

in its ear she went and tried to whisper in its blowhole. Still the whale didn't hear; so she got very cross and said, 'None of this nonsense, now! Let us in at once! I won't have it, do you hear? I simply won't have it!' and she began to stir in his blowhole with her umbrella.

So the whale blew, like an enormous sneeze, and blew her right away up into the sky on top of the water he blew out of his hole, and she was never seen again. So then the nice husband went quietly back to Liverpool.

But the little girl went to the whale's real ear, which was very small and not a bit like his blowhole, and whispered into it, 'Please, nice whale, we would so like to come in, if we may, and live inside.' Then the whale opened his mouth, and the little girl and the Alsatian dog went in.

When they got right down inside, of course, there was no furniture. 'He was quite right,' said the little girl. 'It is certainly not a bit like living in a house.'

The only thing in there was a giant's wig that the whale had once eaten. So the little girl said, 'This will do for a door-mat.' So she made it into a door-mat, and the Alsatian dog went to sleep on it.

When he woke up again he started to dig holes; and of course it gave the whale most terrible pains to have holes dug by such a big dog in his inside, so he went up to the top of the water and shouted to the Captain of a ship to give him a pill. On board the ship there was a cold dressed leg of mutton that the Captain was tired of, so he thought, 'That will make a splendid pill to give the whale.' So he threw it to the whale, and the whale swallowed it; and when it came tobogganing down the whale's throat the Alsatian dog, who was very hungry, ate it, and stopped digging holes; and when the dog stopped digging holes the whale's pain went away. So he said, 'Thank you,' to the Captain. 'That was an excellent pill.'

The Captain was very surprised that his pill had made

the whale well again so soon; he had really only done it to get rid of the cold mutton.

But the poor little girl wasn't so lucky as the Alsatian dog. *He* had a door-mat to sleep on, and something to eat. But there was no bed, and the little girl couldn't sleep without a bed to sleep on possibly, and she had nothing to eat; and this went on for days and days.

Meanwhile the whale began to get rather worried about them. He had swallowed them without thinking much about it; but he soon began to wonder what was happening to them, and whether they were comfortable. He knew nothing at all about little girls. He thought she would probably want something to eat by now, but he didn't know at all what. So he tried to talk down into his own inside, to ask her. But that is very difficult; at any rate *he* couldn't do it. The words all came out instead of going in.

So he swam off to the tropics, where he knew a parrot, and asked him what to do. The parrot said it was quite simple, and flew off to an island where there was a big snake. He bit off its head and bit off its tail, and  then flew back to the whale with the rest of it. He put most of the snake down the whale's throat, so that one end just came up out of its mouth.

'There,' he said, 'now you have got a speaking tube. You speak into one end of the snake, and the words will go down it inside you.'

So the whale said, 'Hallo,' into one end of the snake, and the little girl heard 'Hallo' come out of the other.

'What do you want?' said the whale. 'I want something to eat,' said the little girl. The whale told the parrot, 'She wants something to eat. What do little girls eat?'

'Little girls eat rice pudding,' said the parrot. He had one in a big glass bowl, so he poured it down the snake too, and it came down the other end and the little girl ate it.

When she had eaten it she caught hold of her end of the snake, and called 'Hallo!' up it.

'Hallo!' said the whale.

'May I have a bed?' said the little girl.

'She wants a bed,' the whale said to the parrot.

'You go to Harrods for that,' said the parrot, 'which is the biggest shop in London,' and flew away.

When the whale got to Harrods, he went inside. One of the shopwalkers came up to him and said, 'What can I do for *you*, please?' which sounded very silly.

'I want a bed,' said the whale.

'Mr Binks, BEDS!' the shopwalker called out very loud, and then ran away. He was terribly frightened, because there had never been a whale in the shop before.

Mr Binks the Bed Man came up and looked rather worried.

'I don't know that we have got a bed that will exactly fit you, sir,' he said.

'Why not, silly?' said the whale. 'I only want an ordinary one.'

'Yes, sir,' said the Bed Man, 'but it will have to be rather a large ordinary one, won't it?'

'Of course not, silly,' said the whale. 'On the contrary, it will have to be rather a small one.'

He saw a very nice little one standing in a corner.

'I think that one will just about fit me,' he said.

'You can have it if you like,' said the Bed Man. 'But I think it is you who are the silly to think a little bed like that will fit you!'

'I want it to fit me *inside*, of course,' said the whale, 'not *outside*! – Push!' and he opened his mouth.

So they all came and pushed, and sure enough it did just fit him. Then he ate all the pillow and blankets he could find, which was far more than was needed really, and when it all got down inside, the little girl made the bed and went to sleep on it.

So the whale went back to the sea. Now that the little girl and the Alsatian dog both had had something to eat and somewhere to sleep, they said:

'The man was right, it really is much more fun living in W'ales than living in houses.'

So they stayed on.

PS The parrot went on feeding them, not always on rice pudding.

FROM *THE SPIDER'S PALACE*,
RICHARD HUGHES

FATHER CROCODILE'S CHRISTMAS HIGH

'What's Arthur doing in the shed?' said Father Crocodile to Mother Crocodile.

'I think he's working on our Christmas present,' said Mother.

'O God,' said Father.

'I know what you mean,' said Mother. 'My ribs still ache from when we hit that tree on those motorized tandem skis he made for us last year.'

'Ribs!' said Father. 'If it were only my *ribs*! Sometimes I wish we'd never given him that toolbox.'

'At least he doesn't smoke,' said Mother. 'That's something.'

On Christmas morning the Crocodiles opened their presents. Arthur's sister Emma gave Mother and Father the sweaters she had knitted for them and they gave her a camera. 'I can't wait to take pictures of what comes next,' said Emma. Mother and Father gave Arthur binoculars and a bird book. 'Now I can watch you through the binoculars and look you up in the bird book,' said Arthur. He opened the door of the shed.

'It's a beach umbrella with wheels and a fan,' said Mother.

'We should be so lucky,' said Father. 'It's an aeroplane.'

'It really flies,' said Arthur. He got into the seat, pulled the starter cord, took off, flew once round the house, and landed. He showed Father how to steer and how to make the aeroplane go up and down. 'It's all yours,' he said.

'Better not,' said Mother to Father. 'Remember the motorized skis.'

'It looks like fun,' said Father as he pulled the starter cord and took off.

'Stay over the river!' shouted Mother. 'It's a soft landing and you can always swim home.'

'This is wonderful!' shouted Father from high up in the air. 'How do I get down again?'

'Lean forward,' shouted Arthur.

When Father leaned forward he saw how far down the ground was. He leaned back quickly, the aeroplane climbed sharply and Father stepped out of it into the top of a tall pine tree. He hugged the tree trunk as hard as he could while the aeroplane flew away.

'Come down!' shouted Mother and Emma and Arthur.

'I think I'll just stop here and be quiet for a while,' said Father.

Father stopped in the tree well into the evening. As the moon came up Jimson Crow came along, yawing a little as he flew. 'Hassy Cripmas!' he said to Father.

'Happy Christmas,' said Father.

'What are you going in this wart of the porld?' said Jimson.

'Just getting away from everything for a bit,' said Father. 'You know how it is.'

'Have a drink,' said Jimson, pulling out a hip flask.

'Thanks,' said Father. 'I don't mind if I do.'

'Harpy Crumpus!' said Jimson.

'Harpy Crumpus!' said Father.

RUSSELL HOBAN

SLEEPY SAM

It was a bright morning and Uncle was standing in the moat blowing up water through his trunk between himself and the sun.

'Look, my friends, rainbows!' he called. 'Even Badfort looks tolerable through a rainbow!'

That is one of the good things about being an elephant. You can make fountains and rainbows wherever there is water and sunshine. The moat which surrounds Uncle's vast castle is a particularly good place for doing this. It is fed by seven clear streams, and here and there water foams and leaps into it from the mouths of stone gargoyles. This water comes from lakes which, strange to say, are on top of some of the towers that are grouped together to form the castle.

When Uncle spoke everybody stopped swimming and splashing to look at him. There is nothing Uncle's followers like better than the sight of their leader enjoying himself.

But was he enjoying himself?

Certainly Beaver Hateman's hideous home looked less ugly through a rainbow, but even a rainbow could not disguise the fact that it looked deserted; and whenever Badfort looks deserted it means that the inhabitants are plotting something. No stir of life. No distant shrieks or sounds of glass being smashed. Usually when Uncle bathes in the moat some disreputable person from Badfort comes to sit on the bank and jeer. Nobody was there this morning and Uncle felt increasingly uneasy.

'No doubt those ruffians are licking their wounds,' he said to the Old Monkey. 'It is too early for them to have thought out any new plot, but you might just climb to the top of the drawbridge and see what they're up to.'

'Oh, yes, sir! Can I borrow your field-glasses?'

'They are in the pocket of my dressing-gown on the bank there.'

Uncle finds a purple dressing-gown both dignified and convenient for everyday wear. It falls into majestic folds, and is easy to slip off when he wants to swim.

The Old Monkey jumped out of the water, fetched the glasses, and in no time his thin legs were twinkling up the nearest support of the wooden drawbridge.

Uncle lay back in the water for a minute or two. On his left was the front of Homeward, the part of the castle where he lives with the Old Monkey, the One-Armed Badger, Goodman the cat, Will Shudder the librarian, and two strong guardians, Cloutman and Gubbins. He could also see the nearest of the skyscraper towers, all of different colours and joined by water-chutes and railways. Other towers stand farther back, mysteriously alone, and with no water-chutes or railways . . .

To his right, as he lay there, Uncle could just see the ragged roof and crooked chimneys of Badfort. He could not see the rest of the view, but he knew that beyond Badfort lay the wide stretch of Gaby's Marsh, across which wanders the Badgertown Railway, past Lost Clinkers, the disused gas works, where the gasometer looks like a grey balloon about to collapse, and past Mother Jones's Siding to Badgertown itself. A shabby huddle of a place Badgertown, with Cheapman's Store and the tumbledown palace of the King of the Badgers the only buildings of any size in it. Then beyond Badgertown were deep woods, and beyond those the silver streak of the sea.

As soon as Uncle saw the Old Monkey begin to swing down from cross-bar to cross-bar back to the ground he raised himself out of the water and went to meet him.

'Well?' he asked.

'They're all there, sir.' The Old Monkey sounded worried. 'They're outside the front entrance to Badfort. I could see Beaver Hateman, Nailrod, Filljug, Sigismund, the Wooden-Legged Donkey, Hitmouse and Jellytussle. I couldn't be certain, but I think even Hootman was wavering about!'

'Hootman!' Uncle was startled. 'If you are correct and Hootman is there we can expect trouble very shortly.'

Hootman is the master-spirit behind the Badfort crowd. Nobody knows where he lives, for he is a sort of ghost and comes and goes like a shadow. One thing is certain, whenever Uncle has a really foul plot to contend with it is Hootman who originally thought of it.

'Well, my friend,' said Uncle, 'what else did you see?'

The Old Monkey twisted his paws together unhappily.

'They're playing a sort of game, sir.'

'What sort of game?'

'A . . . a . . . throwing game.'

'Proceed –'

Uncle doesn't often get impatient with the Old Monkey, but he almost did now.

'They've fixed up a big frame with some black cloth stretched over it,' said the Old Monkey, at last. 'They are throwing Black Tom bottles at it!'

'It sounds a mild enough game for them. Was there anything else?'

'There's a sort of drawing on the black cloth, sir.'

'A drawing of what?' trumpeted Uncle, his patience finally giving way.

'An elephant, sir!' whispered the Old Monkey.

'An elephant, you say!' Uncle breathed out heavily. 'Well, never mind, my friend. We must brush such insults off as if they were nothing but spider-webs!'

Goodman, who is very good at finding things out, now came scampering up to Uncle.

'Oh, no, sir,' he said, 'I don't think we ought to brush this off like a spider-web. I think it's important! It's a warning!'

'Goodman,' said Uncle, 'be calm, and explain what you mean.'

Goodman pointed a paw at the stretch of wall behind them.

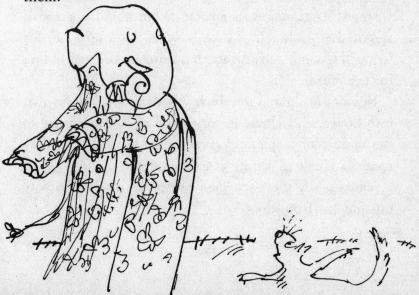

'What about the great mural? Beaver Hateman means to destroy it. They're making a game of it now, but that's what they're planning to do!'

Uncle and his friends looked away from the sparkling waters of the moat to the wall which stretched emptily above their heads. A great mural, showing the life and good works of Uncle, was soon to be painted here. It had been commissioned by the King of the Badgers after the triumph at Crack House. Waldovenison Smeare, the well-known artist, was to start work in a few days.

'Goodman is right, sir,' gasped the Old Monkey. 'They mean to destroy the mural.'

'I fear so,' said Uncle, gravely.

'We must guard it night and day!' said Goodman.

'I agree that some sort of plan must be made,' said Uncle. 'But don't let that villain Beaver Hateman spoil our time of rest and refreshment. The picture isn't painted yet, but, as you say, Goodman, we have been warned! That makes us strong. What about a game of spigots before lunch? I'll be busy in the afternoon, for Cowgill is coming to talk about putting up the scaffolding for the mural.'

Spigots is a game in which wooden balls are thrown into boxes, and Uncle is very good at it. They were in the middle of a splendid game when the Old Monkey came to Uncle in a state of excitement.

'Please, sir, there's a man asleep in a wheelbarrow outside our front door.'

'Nonsense,' said Uncle.

'Come and see, sir. He's very fat and looks very funny!'

Everybody went along to the front door of Homeward, and there, just as the Old Monkey had said, was a vast wheelbarrow, painted red, and in it, lying curled up, was a fat man. He was so fat that his body seemed likely to burst the sides of the barrow. He was snoring gently. A card was pinned to his cap on which were the words SLEEPY SAM. Another card was fastened to his chest:

SLEEPY SAM

GENERAL AGENT

DAY AND NIGHT WATCHING

DON'T WAKE ME

Will discuss terms when

I wake up

DON'T WAKE ME

'A cool customer,' said Uncle. 'A nice way to ask for work, I must say. In any case I can't be bothered with him before lunch.'

'If he wakes I'll say *you're* not to be disturbed, sir,' said the Old Monkey, smiling.

'That's right, pay him back in his own coin,' was Uncle's reply.

Cowgill, Uncle's engineer, who has an engineering shop on the ground floor of one of the towers nearest to Homeward, soon arrived and inspected the wall intended for the painting. He said he had a number of bird apprentices who were very good at flying side by side with light steel bars held in their beaks and that with their help he could put the scaffolding up in no time.

'Mind you,' he said, 'it's going to be a big picture, one hundred feet by thirty. That's a big picture, that is!'

'It has to be seen from a distance,' said Uncle.

'You know who's going to have the best view of it, don't you?' said Cowgill, nodding towards Badfort.

'That had occurred to me,' said Uncle. 'Grateful as I am to my friend the King of the Badgers for his princely gift, I can't help feeling it's going to be a big responsibility.'

'They'll ruin it if they can!' said Cowgill.

As it was such a fine day they were having lunch outside by the moat. Sleepy Sam was still asleep in his wheelbarrow outside the front door.

'Here's Biter, sir,' said the Old Monkey suddenly.

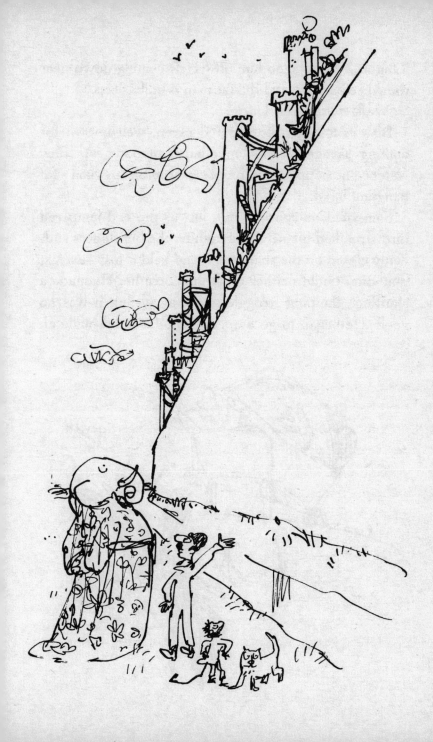

'Oughtn't we to shoo him off? He's coming down near the wheelbarrow, and the fat man is still asleep.'

'Wait!' whispered Uncle.

Biter is a huge, ill-tempered raven, well known for making savage attacks on almost anybody. As they watched he hopped closer and closer to Sleepy Sam's fat dangling hand.

Sam went on snoring, but, just as the bad-tempered bird stretched his neck to bite him, the big fingers suddenly closed on the sharp beak and held it fast – so fast that Biter could neither croak nor breathe. He made a shuffling, flapping struggle to get away, but it was no good. He began to go limp, and the fat hand made an

idle circular movement and tossed him into the moat. The cool water at once revived him, and after some commotion he flew off, casting a glare of rage and fear at the fat snoring figure in the wheelbarrow.

'That was very smartly done,' said Uncle, greatly impressed.

As he spoke the huge figure in the barrow stirred, and the fat hand came up and turned over the card, which now read:

AWAKE AND OPEN TO OFFERS

'I'll have a word with him,' said Uncle.

As Uncle came towards him Sleepy Sam bundled out of the wheelbarrow and made a sort of bow.

'Good morning, sir. Are you the owner of this castle?'

'I am,' said Uncle, 'and I gather you are asking for employment.'

'Yes,' said Sleepy Sam, 'as watchman. No time off, no wages, but two loaves of bread per day and two quarts of Koolvat. I sleep in my barrow.'

'Your terms are most unusual,' said Uncle.

'They suit me,' said Sleepy Sam.

Uncle frowned.

'I conclude you have given the matter full thought. I don't want to employ you and then have you asking for a large salary.'

'I don't want money. I'm rich. Look at these gold

buttons. If I want to buy anything I cut off a button and sell it. They're not easy to steal.'

He held out the front of his enormous coat. It was decorated with two close-set rows of buttons the size of half-crowns and of a dull yellow colour.

'Not at all easy,' agreed Uncle, 'if the way you dealt with the bird Biter is anything to go by. You happen to have turned up when I am particularly in need of a watchman, and I think you may well be the man I want. My staff and myself have a good deal on hand, and can't spend all our time watching the large picture which is shortly to be painted on that stretch of wall there. But it will need watching, for we have reason to believe some people will try to damage it.'

'If you mean that lot,' said Sleepy Sam, waving a hand towards Badfort, 'you couldn't do better than have me. I specialize in watching against Hateman. I know all his tricks.'

'A big claim,' said Uncle, 'but on the evidence of my own eyes I feel inclined to try you. Start at once, and as the day is more than half over you'd better have your wages now.'

The Old Monkey brought Sleepy Sam two large loaves and two quarts of Koolvat. They all watched as he sat in the barrow and ate the loaves, sawing them into thick slices and stuffing each slice whole into his mouth. After he had emptied the cans of Koolvat he got out of the barrow again and waved at Uncle.

'Bye-bye,' he said, and started to trundle the barrow over the drawbridge.

'Strange character,' murmured Uncle, 'but he might well be the person we want.'

'You never know,' said Cowgill, without much confidence.

Next morning Heffo, a strong young mustang who was Uncle's postman, had deposited the usual barrel of letters in Uncle's living-room, and Goodman and the Old Monkey were helping Uncle to deal with his vast correspondence. Uncle owns so much property, and has so many people working for him, that every post brings cheques for rent or for crops of maize and bananas, or else complaints from tenants, most of whom he has never seen. He always hates being disturbed when he is dealing with the post, so he frowned heavily when the light from the window was blocked by a large rough figure which had climbed up on the window-sill.

It was Beaver Hateman, who in the clear light of early morning was a shocking sight. He was wearing a tattered sack suit, and an old top hat above hair which looked like a bundle of badly stacked straw. He carried a stone club under one arm.

'Hi, Unc!' he shouted.

Uncle took off his glasses.

'Will you kindly address me properly,' he said.

'Oh, shut up!' said Hateman. 'You're not getting a lot of bowing and scraping from me! I've come to complain

about that great fat friend of yours who was trespassing on my land last night!"

'I have no fat friend,' said Uncle, with dignity.

'You're lying now, as usual!'

'I have a new employee called Sleepy Sam who might be described as somewhat corpulent!'

'Why can't you talk straight!' snarled Beaver Hateman. 'He's fat, and he's savage. There was Hitmouse, a harmless little fellow if ever I saw one, going home to his little hut outside Badfort when he stumbled over this great snoring bounder in a wheelbarrow. Before he knew it he was stabbed by a skewer! He's very ill this morning with a severe skewer wound in the arm!'

The dwarf Hitmouse is about the most vicious of Beaver Hateman's friends. He is the chief reporter on the *Badfort News*, and always walks about loaded with skewers, intending to stick them into as many people as possible. His most precious possession is a hating book in which he writes down lies about people.

'I gather that Hitmouse has been wounded by one of his own skewers for once,' said Uncle. 'A most salutary lesson!'

'A most salutary lesson!' Hateman mimicked Uncle in a mincing voice. 'Let me tell you I've had enough of your bullying! You pay for your dirty work to be done for you! Well, I'm not a coward! I'm here to make you suffer for that attack on a poor innocent little dwarf!'

Brandishing his stone club, Hateman pushed the window open and was about to jump down into the room. The Old Monkey gave a gasp of fright at this threat to his master, but a large fat hand moved idly into view from below the window-sill and grasping the ragged hem of Hateman's sack suit gave it a sharp tug. The menacing figure was at once jerked back out of sight. A lot of babbling and snarling came from outside. A most revolting noise.

But by the time Uncle, the Old Monkey and Goodman had reached the window, Sleepy Sam seemed to be asleep again in his barrow, and Hateman, kicking up dust and stones, and still yelling with rage, was well on his way back to Badfort.

'Sleepy Sam seems to have begun watching Hateman and his friends already,' said Uncle. 'I think he's going to be an asset.'

FROM *UNCLE AND THE TREACLE TROUBLE*,
J. P. MARTIN

DO-IT-YOURSELF

The Hermit was lying in bed, wondering whether he had the energy to get up. He was usually quite an early riser but life with the Bear was rather exhausting and he couldn't resist the temptation to frowst for just a few more minutes.

He began to let his eyes wander round the cave. It hadn't occurred to him before, but was it perhaps a bit dull and gloomy? 'Perhaps this is the moment for a lick of paint,' he said to himself, wriggling his toes thoughtfully. 'It's a lovely day, and I've got the Bear here to give me a hand.' At this point he wondered whether it *was* such a good idea after all, but as he couldn't think of any other activity to keep the Bear occupied for the day, he came round to deciding that it was too good an opportunity to miss.

When the Bear finally crawled bleary-eyed out of the cave, with a friendly 'Good morning' and a yawn, he was fascinated to see the Hermit sorting through a strange collection of tins and tools and rolls of paper.

The Bear woke up immediately. 'Is that for today's lesson?' he asked, eager to add yet another subject to his list of achievements. 'What are we going to do?'

'Today, I am going to teach you "Do-It-Yourself Home Improvements",' said the Hermit. 'We're going to make this place look really smart.'

The Bear was slightly puzzled as he'd never seen a place look as snug and homely as the Hermit's cave. 'Don't you like it as it is?' he asked.

'Oh, I like it very much,' said the Hermit. 'I wouldn't dream of living anywhere else. But just suppose I ever wanted to sell it and move, eh?'

This reasoning was rather too difficult for the Bear so he said 'Yes' politely.

After breakfast the Hermit began to explain the first job. 'Most of the improvements are needed inside the cave,' he said, 'but there is one very important job to be done outside.'

'What's that, then?' asked the Bear, hopping from foot to foot. The Hermit thought to himself that it might be wiser to start with a job which he could do by himself while the Bear merely stood by and watched, since he was clearly in one of his excitable states. He thought of the well. 'I noticed recently,' said the Hermit, 'that some

of the stones at the well-head are a bit loose. This gives
us a good opportunity to practise Masonry Repairs.' The
Bear couldn't wait to start.

The Hermit mixed a little cement on a wooden board,
took a small trowel, and led the way over to the well.
He leaned over the little wall and peered down.

'Now this stone is loose, you see,' he said, wiggling it
a bit. 'And this one further down. And this one even
further down. Oh dear! It's even worse than I thought.'
By this time he was having to bend right over the parapet.
'I don't think I can reach this last one.'

'Shall I do it, then?' asked the Bear eagerly.

'No!' shouted the Hermit, with a suddenness which made the Bear jump. And he added quickly, 'It's a deep well, my friend, and I wouldn't want you to run the risk of falling down it.' The Bear was very touched that the Hermit was being so considerate.

'You can make yourself useful by giving the handle two or three turns for me while I sit in the bucket and inspect the loose stones.' At this the Hermit squeezed himself into the bucket with his sandalled feet dangling over the edge, while the Bear held the handle firm. 'Now lower me very gently until I say "Stop",' instructed the Hermit.

Perhaps the Bear really was beginning to learn, he thought to himself, as he slowly sank a foot or two. 'Stop!' he called, and the bucket stopped.

The Hermit whistled quietly as he dabbed cement between a few loose stones. 'It's taking more cement than I thought it would,' he called. 'I'll have to come up for another lot.'

Realizing that he could save the Hermit some time, the Bear left the handle and went to scrape up some of the remaining wet cement in his paws. As he did so, he was aware of a strange whirring noise and a very faint cry that sounded rather like 'Aaaargh!', followed by an equally faint splash.

When he got back to the well, the Hermit had gone. The Bear leaned over the well and peered into the darkness. From the depths a distant voice called, 'Wind me up, you nincompoop!'

Obviously the Hermit had gone down to get some water and was now ready to get back to work. The Bear supposed that a nincompoop must be a masonry repairer's assistant, because there wasn't anybody else around. With an effort he brought the Hermit, dripping and gasping, up to the level of the wall again.

'Thirsty work, masonry repairing,' said the Bear, sociably, as the Hermit seemed to be having some difficulty in speaking, 'Oh, I've just remembered: I've got this pile of cement for you,' he added, letting go of the handle and scraping up the cement from the ledge where he'd placed it.

The Hermit couldn't have heard him because he apparently decided to go down the well again. 'Probably remembered he left his trowel down there,' thought the Bear.

'Give a shout when you want to come up again,' he called down the well, helpfully. He was answered by a sound from the bottom of the well, but as it was more like gargling than ordinary speech, he couldn't exactly make out what the Hermit was saying. Still, he thought it best to wind him up.

The Hermit climbed out of the bucket absolutely drenched ('I'm glad I'm not the only clumsy one,' thought the Bear to himself) and, between gasps, explained that he was going to take the rest of the morning off to dry his clothes out, and that the Bear had, in any case, sufficiently mastered all that he was ever going to know about masonry repairs. The Bear glowed with pride at this compliment, and wondered whether he'd be as successful in the afternoon session.

*

The Hermit felt much more relaxed after lunch. The sun was shining and his nerves were in a better state. The Bear was restless, however, and kept rocking backwards and forwards on his log, saying 'Ho ho!' as he often did when he was excited.

'He won't settle down until I give him a job to do,' thought the Hermit to himself. Then he remembered how cheerless he'd thought the inside of the cave had looked that morning. It seemed a pity not to get a little bit of decorating done while the Bear was so keen.

'On your feet, Bear!' he said, springing into action. 'Time to get back to work.'

With this, he led the Bear over to a little trestle table which he had set up on the grass. Under the table, on the ground, was a large pot of paste with a broad brush in it, and on the table was a roll of wallpaper.

The Hermit uncurled the end of the wallpaper, which had a bold pattern of red and white stripes. 'Do you like it?' he asked. The Bear did, very much. 'Come into the cave and you'll see why I chose this particular pattern,' said the Hermit.

He carried the roll to the far end of the cave where the ceiling sloped down so much that the Bear always had to stoop. The Hermit unrolled a length of the paper and held it against the bumpy rock wall.

'One reason why I chose this paper is that up-and-down stripes always make a room taller,' he said. He didn't add that another reason was that this was the only

paper he possessed, because he didn't want to confuse the Bear with too many reasons at once. 'You'll admit that the ceiling is rather low just here.'

The Bear admitted it readily, remembering the number of times, in his early days in the cave, when he'd stood up suddenly and bumped his head. 'Well, this makes the ceiling higher,' explained the Hermit. The Bear was very grateful for this and stood up straight to take the weight off his bended knees. He bumped his head on the ceiling. Obviously the paper only altered the height of the ceiling when it was properly stuck on the wall.

'And now I'll show you how to paste the paper,' said the Hermit, trotting out to the table again. The prospect of doing some useful work made the Bear forget his bump, and he rubbed his paws together with a chuckle.

With great skill and confidence, considering he'd never done anything like it before, the Hermit laid the wallpaper face down on the trestle table and slapped a quantity of paste on to it. 'There,' he said, 'you just finish that while I give the wall a quick dusting.' And he took his dustpan and brush and popped back into the cave. He was looking forward to improving his home as much as the Bear was.

With immense concentration, because it was a great responsibility, the Bear took the broad brush in both paws – the only way he could hold it steadily – and tried to spread paste on the wallpaper. But he found it very hard to control the brush as the paste made it stick to the paper.

Fortunately he had a bright idea. The brush was made of hair, and so was the back of his paw; so he simply dipped his paw into the can and flopped it backwards and forwards across the paper. It made a very satisfying noise.

When the paper was sufficiently awash with paste, the
Bear decided to do the other side. Singing quietly to
himself, he lifted the paper and turned it over (no easy
job, that) and flopped away a bit more. Unluckily, the
dangling ends of the paper kept getting themselves
wrapped around the Bear's legs, and when he managed
to unpeel them, in a rather crinkled state, they then
started wrapping themselves around the legs of the
trestle table.

At first the Bear was distressed because he thought
he might be messing things up, but when he stood back

and saw how much more colourful the old trestle table looked covered in red and white stripes, he felt that that was probably what the Hermit had had in mind for the second job of the afternoon. What's more, there was plenty of paper still rolled up for the cave wall.

Some old scraps of paper which had got extra soggy and had fallen off bothered him a bit, until he realized that he could use them to cover the Hermit's favourite rock seat and his own log. The paper had got itself so rumpled that it was difficult to preserve the up-and-down movement of the stripes – in fact, some of the stripes were very definitely side-to-side – but the general effect was so smart and eye-catching that he knew the Hermit would be pleased.

The Bear was working hard at the rather difficult task of wallpapering a tree without wallpapering himself too much, when the Hermit breezed out of the cave with his dustpan and brush. He froze when he saw the results of the Bear's efforts.

'I thought you'd like it,' said the Bear. 'It makes the table much higher of course, but I can still reach it. Shall I paper the wall in the cave now, or do you want me to finish the trees first?'

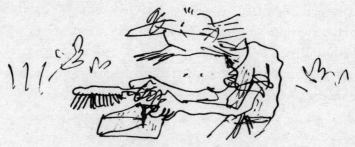

'No, Bear,' the Hermit said quietly. 'You've passed what we call the "papier-mâché" part of the test (the Bear hadn't realized that it was so important) and, in any case, you appear to have used up most of the wall-paper.' The Hermit made a mental note to include Paper-Stripping among the Bear's studies at a later date.

A little while after, the Bear sat playing with the Hermit's plastic boats in the tin tub while the Hermit did his best to wash the remaining traces of paste and paper from his fur.

'Did we finish the Home Improvement,' asked the Bear, 'or have we got to carry on tomorrow?'

Behind the Bear's back the Hermit gave an involuntary shudder. 'Oh, no,' he said. 'I've been thinking it over, you know, and really and truly I prefer the cave as it is.'

And really and truly he meant it.

FROM *THE HERMIT AND THE BEAR*,
JOHN YEOMAN

THE LIQUORICE TREE

Old Mrs Abelsea had very regular habits.

'You *got* to have,' she said, 'to get all the work done *and* bring up two grandsons.'

The grandsons were called Mat and Rod. Their mother was a sailor, their father was a merman, in fact the king of the sea. So it was Mrs Abelsea who looked after the boys. Their mother came home at the end of every trip. But sometimes the trips lasted for months and months.

Every morning at seven, Mrs Abelsea got up, went outside, nodded to the morning star, waved to the rooks tumbling round the church tower, and milked the goat. Then she fed the hens and listened to the radio news.

At eight she gave the boys their breakfast: boiled eggs and buttered toast.

'You'll have to keep a lookout, today, on the way to school,' she said, one morning. 'On the eight o'clock news it was. Martians tipped a load of Gondwana beasts all around our village. You better watch out for them.'

'*Gondwana beasts?*'

Both boys stopped eating in mid-egg.

'Beasts like they used to have in Gondwana-land, millions of years ago.' Mrs Abelsea pressed her lips together and shook her head. 'The Martians have got them now it seems. And want to get rid of them. Giant snakes, toothy bat-birds, polacanthus, spike-backed tapirs, iguanodons, astrapotheria, mammoths and the like. What *right* do they have to dump their unwanted monsters here? Answer me that?'

Now they could all hear shrill screeches and whistling overhead. There were loud thumps from the village green.

'Finish your eggs first!' said Mrs Abelsea. The boys were wild to get outside. 'And then make your beds, *brush your teeth*, put your homework and packed lunches in your schoolbags – you'll have plenty of time to look at the monsters while you wait for the school bus.'

After she had put away the breakfast dishes, Mrs Abelsea always walked three times barefoot round the village green. This was to keep up its rating as a piece of Common Land, where the villagers could pasture their goats and geese. 'Otherwise,' as Mrs Abelsea said, 'some glib-gab is going to build houses over it before you can blow your nose.'

Today, as she walked round the green, Mrs Abelsea noticed an astrapotherium sharpening its snout on the letter box. It was a large hoofed beast of very odd appearance. An aardvark was thoughtfully chewing on a motorbike. A polacanthus, with a row of spikes along its back, was sucking up the contents of a litter bin.

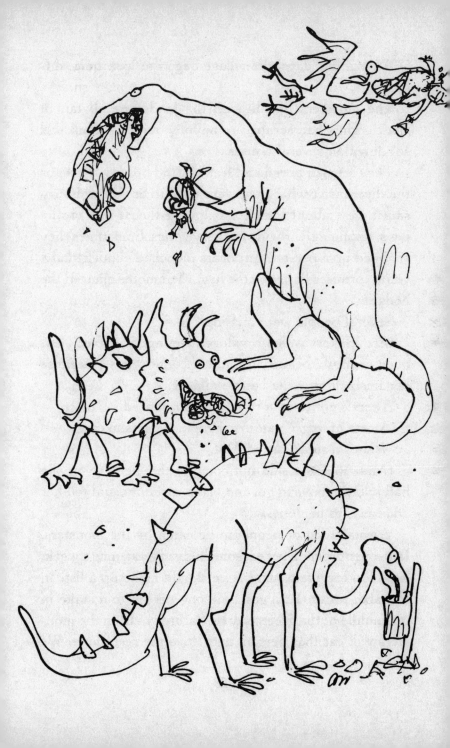

After a few days, the village began to look quite different.

The monsters had heaved the landscape all out of shape. They had scraped some hills quite flat, and had sat down on several houses.

They seemed bored and fretful. And hungry. Perhaps the diet wasn't what they were used to on Mars. Pterosauria flew about the sky, snapping their great toothy jaws, flapping their wide leathery wings. Sometimes they snapped up a person. Ant bears mooched about glumly. Giant tortoises flattened the hay. Mammoths chewed the hedges.

Several people went missing.

Mrs Vickers called a village meeting. She lived next door to Mrs Abelsea, in a much bigger house, because her husband was the bank manager.

'There's got to be a rota,' she announced.

'A rota of *what*?' said Mr Brook, the postman.

'What's a rota?' asked Mat.

(Mrs Abelsea could not come to the meeting, so she had told the boys to go, and listen carefully, and tell her what was to be done.)

'A rota, a list of people to be eaten by the monsters. In proper order. They eat somebody at least once a week. So – to keep them quiet – we should make up a list. In alphabet order, I suggest. Tie one person to a stake in the middle of the green, say on Saturday. Then the monsters will eat that person, and leave the rest alone. We

can start with the names of people who begin with A,'
said Mrs Vickers, giving Mat and Rod a nasty look.

Mat and Rod had never got on well with the six
Vickers boys, who were called Ben and Len, Ted and
Ned, Tom, and Urk. The Vickers boys liked fooling
about. This nearly always ended in somebody's car getting smashed. Rod and Mat liked making things. Every
now and then, the Vickers boys smashed up the things
that Rod and Mat had made.

'But suppose everybody in the village gets eaten?' said
Mr Young, the parish clerk. 'Then what'll we do?'

'Oh, the Government is sure to have done something
by then,' said Mrs Vickers.

Since no one had a better plan, Mrs Vickers's idea
was agreed to.

'We'll start next Saturday,' said Mr Young. 'Anyway,

that'll be one less on the school bus.' And he wrote down 'Mat Abelsea'.

The boys went home to tea, and told their grandmother what had been decided.

Now the reason she was not able to come to the meeting was that, every day, exactly at 3.41 in the afternoon, she Listened.

'There is one quiet minute, every day, just at that time,' she had told the boys. 'And if you listen hard, sometimes you get good advice.'

'Who from, Grandma?' the boys asked.

'It's the voice of the Old Ones,' she told them. 'I can hear it; and my old grannie used to hear it; and you boys will hear it by and by, if you grow to be my age.'

But it looked as if the boys never *would* grow to be her age, as their names were first on the list to be eaten by monsters.

Luckily, on this particular afternoon, when she was listening, the Old Ones had spoken to Mrs Abelsea.

'Why not ring up Mars?' they said.

'Ring up Mars, how can we ring up Mars?' Mrs Abelsea grumbled. But Mat and Rod, who were very clever with old bits of wire, and flint, and fibreglass, and sardine tins saw no problem about that. They made an X-band, solar-beamed, polarized radiophone out of coffee jars, pill bottles, breadcrumbs and the elastic bands the postman dropped on the front doorstep.

Mat rang up Mars and asked for the Controller.

'Mars Head Office here, yes? Can I help you?'

'Look, we are having a lot of trouble from all those monsters you dumped on our village. Can you take them back?'

'So, sorry, so, sorry,' said the Controller of Mars. He sounded as if he had a mouthful of Martian marbles. That was because of the interstellar translation screen. 'Was a bad mistake to dump them. Due to wrongly spelt office memo. Said *Earth*, should have said *Earda*. Earda is a small moon of Venus where no one lives. So, sorry, will not happen again.'

'But it's happened *now*, and people are being eaten, and all our hills and trees are being heaved about. Will you take the monsters back?'

'So, sorry, so, sorry. Not possible. Monster-dumping

is one-way. No way to reverse. Have a nice day.'

'Well – at least – tell us, how can we get rid of them?' shouted Mat.

'Try sound. Try unnatural sound. Monsters not hear such sounds before. Have a nice day.'

'Unnatural sound. What's *that*?' muttered Mat, thumping down the receiver.

'Umn?' said Rod. He was building a statue of a wild boar. It was made from a car sump, a lobster-pot, a traffic bollard, and a basket of huge nails. He was very busy.

'*You're* all right,' said Mat crossly. 'I come before you in the alphabet. You have two weeks. I only have one. What is unnatural sound?'

Rod picked up a bit of copper pipe which the gas man had given him, and rattled it along the row of nails on the back of his boar's neck:

TRR-ING-NG-NG-NG-NG-IIIINNNNGGGG.

'Music,' he said. 'This is where we have to get together with the Vickers lot.'

'*Them*? What do they know about music?'

'Sweet silver nothing. But we'll have to teach them.'

Rod and Mat went to see their enemies, the Vickers boys, who, as usual, were drinking root beer and playing a game called Drop Dead in Farmer Gostrey's barn.

'Hey, you dwergs, what you doin' here?' yelled Ben Vickers, who was the lookout. 'Frog off! We don't want nothin' to do with you little swickers!'

'Mat this week, ho, ho, Rod next, har har,' shouted

Urk over his brother's shoulder. 'Soon the monsters'll have ye. Chomp chomp!'

Urk was the biggest and roughest and toughest of the Vickers boys.

'Yes, and who's the week after? You!' said Rod. 'I've seen old Young's list. He's got your Dad down as Mr *Adsett*-Vickers. So you come after us.'

'*What????*'

'Yes! It's so. So listen! We've got a plan. Want to hear it?'

As Rod spoke, a pterosaurus flapped overhead, snapping its razor-sharp jaws. Urk and Ben turned pale.

'Hey, you'd better come in the barn. No sense waiting for an ant bear to come and knock you off. Has old Young *really* got our family down as Adsett-Vickers?'

'Here's the list, look.'

But none of the Vickers boys could read.

'Well, listen. This is what we've got to do,' said Rod. 'We've got to start a band. An Iron Band. A Cast-iron Band. That'll be *really* rough sound. We want to make trumpets, bugles, drums, fifes, cymbals. And we haven't much time to make them. Let alone practise on them.'

'*Practise?*' said Urk, looking disgusted, but Ben said, 'Hey! Our Mum's got a set of bagpipes.'

'What'll we make drums *from*?'

'There's an old water tank on wheels in the field behind,' Ted suddenly spoke up. 'Old Gostrey won't kick up if we take it. He got eaten yesterday by an aardvark.'

The tank on wheels, when cut up, gave them enough metal for several drums, of different sizes. They made bugles from water-sprinklers. The cutting blades of ploughs were rolled up to make trumpets. Old Mrs Abelsea's grannie's warming-pan gave them a fine pair of cymbals. Rod learned to play the bagpipes.

The Vickers boys had never worked so hard in their lives before. As soon as they had real trumpets, bugles, and cymbals to play on, they became as keen as mustard.

Evenings were spent practising in the barn.

Old Mrs Abelsea had a song that she always sang when cutting up carrots.

Skillo-me, skillo-my, throw your peelings into the sky,
Skillery-my, skillery-me, throw the rinds in the liquorice
  tree.

It went to a very cheerful tune, so they practised at that. By Saturday, they could all play it pretty well, except Urk, who never came in on time.

'But that doesn't matter,' said Rod. 'Just so long as we make plenty of noise.'

On Saturday they started out in a procession round the village green. The stake was already in place, out in the middle. Mrs Vickers had seen to that. And now she was lurking in the phone box, hoping to see Mat tied to it and snapped up by a mammoth.

Plenty of monsters were about. Indeed the music seemed to bring them from all over the district, like wasps to jam: giant tortoises, dinosaurs, triceratops, and toothy bat-birds. They hung and trundled and swooped and flapped, they roared and wailed and honked and boomed. More and more came, from further and further away.

But the music was louder than all of them.

'*Give it all you've got, boys!*' yelled Rod, pounding away on his huge drums, and then blowing the bagpipes till his ears stood out sideways. Ben and Len blew trumpets. Urk whanged on the cymbals. Tom screeched on the fife. Ned and Ted were the buglers. Mat had kettledrums and a mouth-organ made from an old toaster, which he played at the same time as he banged his drums.

The noise they made was ear-splitting. Lots of people in the village complained. Mr Young declared that it was an outrage. He was going to write to *The Times*, he said. So did Mr Brook and old Mrs Pinpye.

But Mrs Abelsea said, 'Look, I think some of the monsters are beginning to shrink.'

It was true, they were. Like leaky balloons, they drooped and dwindled. They sighed and sagged. They flickered and flopped. And, at last – by now they were only the size of teacups – they just simply lay down and died.

'Now we've got to bury them all,' grumbled Mr Young.

❋

After that, the boys kept their band going. But they had to find a barn miles and miles away from the village to practise in, because of the complaints from Mr Young and Mr Vickers. (Mrs Vickers, in the phone box, had been sat on by an iguanodon, just before he began to shrink.) And Urk, oddly enough, shrank just as fast as the monsters did, and, in the end, vanished entirely.

Mat rang up Mars to say that unnatural noise had done the job.

'Very, happy,' said Mars politely. 'Have a nice day.'

Mrs Abelsea said, 'You see? It all comes of having regular habits.'

FROM *THE WINTER SLEEPWALKER*,
JOAN AIKEN

THE CRAYFISH BROUGHT TO JUSTICE

One day a crayfish happened to turn up in Schilda. Nobody knew where it had come from or what it wanted among the people of Schilda. And as they had never seen a crayfish before in their lives they got terribly excited.

They sounded the alarm on their new church bell, rushed to the place where the crayfish was crawling about and ... had no idea what to do. They made all kinds of guesses, trying to work out what it was they were dealing with – they did so want to know. 'Perhaps it's a tailor,' said the Burgomaster, 'otherwise why would it have two pairs of scissors?'

Already someone had gone to look for a piece of cloth. He put the crayfish on it and exclaimed: 'If you're a tailor, then cut me out a jacket! With wide sleeves and

a collar!' The creature wandered to and fro across the cloth, but it didn't cut it out. So the master-tailor of Schilda took his own big scissors and cut the cloth exactly following the lines of the movements of the crayfish. At the end of ten minutes the material was completely hacked to pieces. There was no question of a jacket with wide sleeves and a collar. 'My beautiful expensive cloth!' wailed the Schildburgher. 'This fellow is having us on! He isn't a tailor at all! I'm going to have him up for damage to property!'

Then he put out his hand towards the crayfish to push it aside. But the crayfish got hold of his hand and pinched him so hard with its claws that the man yelled with pain. 'Murder!' he screamed. 'Murder! Help!'

By now the Burgomaster had had enough. 'First it ruins this expensive cloth,' he said, 'and now it makes an attempt on the life of one of our fellow-citizens. As the chief dignitary of the town, that is something I cannot allow. Tomorrow we shall put it on trial!'

And so it was. In a formal session of the court the crayfish was charged by the judge with malicious damage and attempted murder. Eyewitnesses described on oath

what had occurred the previous day. The officially appointed defence counsel were able to submit no exonerating evidence.

The court withdrew briefly to consider its verdict and then delivered the following severe but just sentence:

'The malefactor is deemed guilty on both counts in the indictment. Extenuating circumstances can the less be taken into consideration, since the defendant is not locally resident and has ill repaid the hospitality accorded him. He is condemned to death. He will be drowned by the bailiff. This verdict is not subject to appeal. The costs of the proceedings will be borne by the municipal treasury.'

The very same afternoon the bailiff carried the crayfish to the lake in a basket and lobbed it in a wide curve into the water.

Everyone in Schilda was present at the execution. The women had tears in their eyes. 'That won't do any good,' said the Burgomaster. 'Punishment there's got to be.'

The clergyman, incidentally, had not come with them. He didn't know if the crayfish was Catholic or Protestant.

ERICH KÄSTNER

HOW THE RHINOCEROS
GOT HIS SKIN

Once upon a time, on an uninhabited island on the shores of the Red Sea, there lived a Parsee from whose hat the rays of the sun were reflected in more-than-oriental splendour. And the Parsee lived by the Red Sea with nothing but his hat and his knife and a cooking-stove of the kind that you must particularly never touch. And one day he took flour and water and currants and plums and sugar and things, and made himself one cake which was two feet across and three feet thick. It was indeed a Superior Comestible (*that's* Magic), and he put it on the stove because *he* was allowed to cook on that stove, and he baked it and he baked it till it was all done brown and smelt most sentimental. But just as he was going to eat it there came down to the beach from the Altogether Uninhabited Interior one Rhinoceros with a horn on his nose, two piggy eyes, and few manners. In those days the Rhinoceros's skin fitted him quite tight. There were no wrinkles in it anywhere. He looked exactly like a Noah's Ark Rhinoceros, but of course much bigger. All the same, he had no manners then, and he has no manners now, and he never will have any manners. He said, 'How!' and the Parsee left that cake

and climbed to the top of a palm-tree with nothing on but his hat, from which the rays of the sun were always reflected in more-than-oriental splendour. And the Rhinoceros upset the oil-stove with his nose, and the cake rolled on the sand, and he spiked that cake on the horn of his nose, and he ate it, and he went away, waving his tail, to the desolate and Exclusively Uninhabited Interior which abuts on the islands of Mazanderan, Socotra, and the Promontories of the Larger Equinox. Then the Parsee came down from his palm-tree and put the stove on its legs and recited the following *Sloka*, which, as you have not heard, I will now proceed to relate:

> 'Them that takes cakes
> Which the Parsee-man bakes
> Makes dreadful mistakes.'

And there was a great deal more in that than you would think.

Because, five weeks later, there was a heat-wave in the Red Sea, and everybody took off all the clothes they had. The Parsee took off his hat; but the Rhinoceros took off his skin and carried it over his shoulder as he came down to the beach to bathe. In those days it buttoned underneath with three buttons and looked like a waterproof. He said nothing whatever about the Parsee's cake, because he had eaten it all; and he never had any manners, then since, or hence-forward. He waddled

straight into the water and blew bubbles through his nose, leaving his skin on the beach.

Presently the Parsee came by and found the skin, and he smiled one smile that ran all round his face two times. Then he danced three times round the skin and rubbed his hands. Then he went to his camp and filled his hat with cake-crumbs, for the Parsee never ate anything but cake, and never swept out his camp. He took that skin, and he shook that skin, and he scrubbed that skin, and he rubbed that skin just as full of old, dry, stale, tickly cake-crumbs and some burned currants as ever it could *possibly* hold. Then he climbed to the top of his palm-tree and waited for the Rhinoceros to come out of the water and put it on.

And the Rhinoceros did. He buttoned it up with the three buttons, and it tickled like cake-crumbs in bed. Then he wanted to scratch, but that made it worse; and then he lay down on the sands and rolled and rolled and rolled, and every time he rolled the cake-crumbs tickled

him worse and worse and worse. Then he ran to the palm-tree and rubbed and rubbed and rubbed himself against it. He rubbed so much and so hard that he rubbed his skin into a great fold over his shoulders, and another fold underneath, where the buttons used to be (but he rubbed the buttons off), and he rubbed some more folds over his legs. And it spoiled his temper, but it didn't make the least difference to the cake-crumbs. They were inside his skin and they tickled. So he went home, very angry indeed and horribly scratchy; and from that day to this every rhinoceros has great folds in his skin and a very bad temper, all on account of the cake-crumbs inside.

But the Parsee came down from his palm-tree, wearing his hat, from which the rays of the sun were reflected in more-than-oriental splendour, packed up his cooking-stove, and went away in the direction of Orotavo, Amygdala, the Upland Meadows of Antananarivo, and the Marshes of Sonaput.

FROM *JUST SO STORIES*,
RUDYARD KIPLING

FIRST-CLASS SNAKE STORIES

'Do you want some items about snakes?' asked an agriculturally rural-looking gentleman of the *Eagle*'s city editor the other day.

'If they are fresh and true,' responded the city editor.

'Exactly,' replied the farmer. 'These items are both. Nobody knows 'em but me. I got a farm down on the island a piece, and there's lots of snakes on it. Near the house is a pond, about six feet deep. A week ago my little girl jumped into the pond, and would have drowned if it hadn't been for a snake. The snake seen her, went for her, and brought her ashore. The particular point about this item is the way he did it.'

'How was it?' asked the city editor.

'It was a black snake, about thirty feet long, and he just coiled the middle of himself around her neck so she couldn't swallow any water, and swum ashore with his head and tail. Is that a good item?'

'First-class.'

'You can spread it out, you know. After they got ashore the girl patted the snake *on the* head, and it went off pleased as Punch. Ever since then he comes to the house regular at meal-times, and she feeds him on pie. Think you can make anything out of that item?'

'Certainly. Know any more?'

'Yes. I got a baby six months old. He's a boy. We generally sit him out on the grass of a morning, and he hollers like a bull all day; at least he used to, but he don't any more. One morning we noticed he wasn't hollering, and wondered what was up. When we looked, there was a rattlesnake coiled up in front of him scanning his features. The boy was grinning and the snake was grinning. Bimeby the snake turned his tail to the baby and backed his rattle right into the baby's fist.'

'What did the baby do?'

'Why, he just rattled that tail so you could hear it three-quarters of a mile, and the snake lay there and grinned. Every morning we found the snake there, until one day a bigger snake came, and the baby played with his rattle just the same till the first snake came back. He looked thin, and I reckon he had been sick and sent the other to take his place. Will that do for an item?'

'Immensely,' replied the city editor.

'You can fill in about the confidence of childhood and all that, and you might say something about the blue-eyed cherub. His name is Isaac. Put that in to please my wife.'

'I'll do it. Any more snake items?'

'Lemme see. You've heard of hoop-snakes?'

'Yes, often.'

'Just so. Not long ago we heard a fearful row in our cellar one night. It sounded like a rock-blast, and then there was a hiss and things was quiet. When I looked in the morning the cider barrel had busted. But we didn't lose much cider.'

'How did you save it?'

'It seems that the staves had busted out, but before they could get away, four hoop-snakes coiled around the barrel and tightened it up and held it together until we drew the cider off in bottles. That's the way we found 'em, and we've kept 'em around the house ever since. We're training 'em for shawl-straps now. Does that strike you favorably for an item?'

'Enormously!' responded the city editor.

'You can fix it up so as to show how quick they was to get there before the staves were blown off. You can work in the details.'

'Of course. I'll attend to that. Do you think of any more?'

'Ain't you got enough? Lemme think. Oh, yes! One Sunday me and my wife was going to church, and she dropped her garter somewhere. She told me about it, and I noticed a little striped snake running alongside and listening to her. Bimeby he made a spring and just wound himself around her stocking, or tried to, but he didn't fetch it.'

'Why not?'

'He wasn't quite long enough. He jumped down and shook his head and started off. We hadn't gone more'n a quarter of a mile, when we see him coming out of the woods just ahead of us. He was awful hot and tired, and he had another snake with him twice as big as he was.

They looked at my wife a minute and said something to each other, and then the big snake went right to the place where the garter belonged. He wrapped right around it, put his tail in his mouth and went to sleep. We got him yet. We use him to hold the stovepipe together when we put the stove up. Is that any use as an item?'

'Certainly,' said the city editor.

'You can say something about the first snake's eye for distances and intellectuality, when he found he wouldn't go 'round. You know how to do that better than me.'

'I'll give him the credit he deserves. Can you tell us any more?'

'I don't call any to mind just at present. My wife knows a lot of snake items, but I forget 'em. By the way, though, I've got a regular living curiosity down at my place. One day my oldest boy was sitting on the back stoop doing his sums, and he couldn't get 'em right. He felt something

against his face, and there was a little snake coiled up on his shoulder and looking at the slate. In four minutes he had done all them sums. We've tamed him so he keeps all our accounts, and he is the lightningest cuss at figures you ever seen. He'll run up a column eight feet long in three seconds. I wouldn't take a reaper for him.'

'What kind of a snake is he?' inquired the editor, curiously.

'The neighbors call him an adder.'

'Oh, yes, yes!' said the city editor, a little disconcerted. 'I've heard of the species. When did all these things happen?'

'Along in the fore part of the spring, but I didn't say anything about 'em, 'cause it wasn't the season for snake items. This is about the time for that sort of thing, isn't it?'

'Yes,' chipped in the exchange editor, 'you couldn't have picked out a better time for snake stories.'

ANON.

CAPTAIN CAP AND A MUSICAL INTERLUDE

Last Sunday at the races I ran into Captain Cap, which was all the more delightful since I was under the impression that our engaging navigator was in port in Bilbao. That day isn't yet so lost in the mists of time that anyone has forgotten how appalling the weather was.

'Wet is as wet does,' concluded Cap, after we had exchanged greetings. 'If something is going to get wet I'd rather it were my throat in the Australian Wine Store.[1] What do you think?'

'Splendid idea, Captain.'

'Well, let's go.'

We went.

'What will it be, gentlemen?' inquired the charming little lady who runs the Australian Wine Store.

'Well now,' said Cap. 'What shall we have?'

'As far as I'm concerned, it rains on my heart as it rains on the city, so I think I'll treat myself to a nice little Angler's Cocktail.'

'What a good idea. I too shall have a nice little Angler's Cocktail.'

It was just at that moment that someone known to

[1] one of our favourite Parisian watering-holes

Cap came into the bar, and was introduced to me. I didn't quite catch his name but, as for his job, if I live as long as several Methuselahs laid end to end, I shall never forget it.

He bore the modest title of Director of Music on the submarine *Goubet* (pride of the French navy).

This strange official started to tell us stories which were stranger still. He had spent the whole summer, he told us, training mussels.

'The mussel in no way deserves its long-standing reputation for stupidity. It's just that you have to treat it very gently, because it's fundamentally a very timid mollusc. With kindness and a little music, you can do anything you like with it.'

'Come on!'

'Cross my heart. As I stand here before you – Captain Cap will tell you I'm not the sort of person to make things up – I managed, while playing Spanish melodies on the guitar, to be accompanied by mussels playing the castanets.'

'No mean achievement!'

'Perhaps I should make it clear . . . I'm not saying that the mussels were actually playing castanets; they *imitated*

220

castanets by clicking their shells together. Very rhythmical they were too. Believe me, gentlemen, there are few sights more entertaining than a rock covered with mussels all keeping perfect time.'

'One has to admit that it can't be an everyday occurrence.'

During the whole of the Director of Music's story Cap hadn't said a word, but he had a restive air about him that did not bode well.

Suddenly he burst out, 'Mussel training, so what! It's child's play! I've seen something ten times better!'

The Director of Music looked a little startled.

'Ten times better? Ten times?'

'A thousand times! In California I saw a chap who had trained birds to land on telegraph wires according to the musical note they represented.'

'I think perhaps a little further explanation is called for.'

'Well, here's how it was. My man chose a telegraph line with five wires, each wire representing the line of a stave. Each bird was trained to represent a C, a D, an E, and so forth. As for the tempo, the white birds were the white notes, the black birds the black ones, the little birds were the quavers and the even smaller ones were the semiquavers. That's as far as my chap went.'

'Not bad, even so.'

'This is how he did it. He arrived where the performance was to take place with huge baskets full of birds.

After he had opened one special little basket, he indicated the key he wanted for the piece. A grass snake came out of the special little basket, curled itself round the telegraph pole and slithered up to the wires, where it shaped itself into a key of F or a key of G. Then the man started to play the piece on a wickerwork trombone.'

'Sorry to interrupt you, Cap. A trombone made of what?'

'Wickerwork. You must be aware that Californian peasants are expert in the craft of making trombones of wickerwork?'

'When I was in California I was only passing through. Unfortunately I had no time to dwell on ethnographic details.'

'Well, at each note from the instrument, a bird flew off and landed in the right place. When everybody was in position, the concert began, each of our little feathered friends emitting its note in turn.'

The charming little lady who runs the Australian Wine Store seemed entranced by such an imaginative fantasy; and as we were showing some signs of doubt about the whole business, she took it upon herself to fly to the Captain's assistance with the following solemn observation:

'Everything he says is absolutely true, you know. I saw all the little musical creatures with my own eyes. On the telegraph wires from Cornpone to Blonxville – that was it, wasn't it, Cap?'

ALPHONSE ALLAIS

THE SEAL WHO BECAME FAMOUS

A seal who lay basking on a large, smooth rock said to himself: all I ever do is swim. None of the other seals can swim any better than I can, he reflected, but, on the other hand, they can all swim just as well. The more he pondered the monotony and uniformity of his life, the more depressed he became. That night he swam away and joined a circus.

Within two years the seal had become a great balancer. He could balance lamps, billiard cues, medicine balls, hassocks, taborets, dollar cigars, and anything else you

gave him. When he read in a book a reference to the Great Seal of the United States, he thought it meant him. In the winter of his third year as a performer he went back to the large, smooth rock to visit his friends and family. He gave them the Big Town stuff right away: the latest slang, liquor in a golden flask, zippers, a gardenia in his lapel. He balanced for them everything there was on the rock to balance, which wasn't much. When he had run through his repertory, he asked the other seals if they could do what he had done and they all said no. 'OK,' he said. 'Let's see you do something I can't do.' Since the only thing they could do was swim, they all plunged off the rock into the sea. The circus seal plunged right after them, but he was so hampered by his smart city clothes, including a pair of seventeen-dollar shoes, that he began to founder at once. Since he hadn't been in swimming for three years, he had forgot what to do with his flippers and tail, and he went down for the third time before the other seals could reach him: they gave him a simple but dignified funeral.

Moral: Whom God has equipped with flippers should not monkey around with zippers.

FROM *FABLES FOR OUR TIME*,
JAMES THURBER

A SENSIBLE VARMINT

Almost every boddy that knows the forrest, understands parfectly well that Davy Crockett never loses powder and ball, havin' ben brort up to blieve it a sin to throw away amminition, and that is the bennefit of a vartuous eddikation. I war out in the forrest won arternoon, and had jist got to a plaice called the grate gap, when I seed a rakkoon setting all alone upon a tree. I klapped the breech of Brown Betty to my sholder, and war jist a going to put a piece of led between his sholders, when he lifted one paw, and sez he, 'Is your name Crockett?'

Sez I, 'You are rite for wonst, my name is Davy Crockett.'

'Then,' sez he, 'you needn't take no further trubble, for I may as well cum down without another word'; and the cretur wauked rite down from the tree, for he considered himself shot.

I stoops down and pats him on the head, and sez I, 'I hope I may be shot myself before I hurt a hare of your head, for I never had sich a kompliment in my life.'

'Seeing as how you say that,' sez he, 'I'll jist walk off for the present, not doubting your word a bit, d'ye see, but lest you should kinder happen to change your mind.'

ANON.

THE LEGEND OF MIMIR

It is a beautiful legend of the Norse land. Amilias was the village blacksmith, and under the spreading chestnut treekjn, his village smithophjken stood. He the hot iron gehammered and sjhod horses for fifty cents all round please. He made tin hjelmets for the gjodds, and stove pjipe trousers for the hjeroes.

Mimir was a rival blacksmith. He didn't go in very much for defensive armor, but he was lightning on two-edged Bjswords and cut-and-slash svjcutlassssses. He made chyjeese kjnives for the gjodds, and he made the great Bjsvsstnsen, an Arkansaw toothpick that would make a free incision clear into the transverse semi-colon of a cast-iron Ichthyosaurus, and never turn its edge. That was the kind of a Bhjairpin Mimir said he was.

One day Amilias made an impenetrable suit of armor for a second-class gjodd, and put it on himself to test it, and boastfully inserted a card in the *Svensska Norderbjravisk jkanaheldesplvtdenskgorodovusaken*, saying that he was wearing a suit of home-made, best-chilled Norway merino underwear, that would nick the unnumbered saw teeth in the pot metal cutlery of the iron-mongery over the way. That, Amilias remarked to his friend Bjohnn Bjrobinssson, was the kind of a Bdjucckk he was.

When Mimir spelled out the card next morning, he said, 'Bjjj!' and went to work with a charcoal furnace, a cold anvil, and the new isomorphic process, and in a little while he came down-street with a sjword, that glittered like a dollar-store diamond, and met Amilias down by the new opera-house. Amilias buttoned on his new Bjarmor and said:

'If you have no hereafter use for your chyjeese kjnife, strike.' Mimir spat on his hands, whirled his skjword above his head and fetched Amilias a swipe that seemed to miss everything except the empty air, through which it softly whistled. Amilias smiled, and said 'go on,' adding that it 'seemed to him he felt a general sense of cold iron somewhere in the neighborhood, but he hadn't been hit.'

'Shake yourself,' said Mimir.

Amilias shook himself, and immediately fell into halves, the most neatly divided man that ever went beside himself.

'That's where the boiler-maker was away off in his diagnosis,' said Mimir, as he went back to his shop to put up the price of cutlery 65 per cent in all lines, with an unlimited advance on special orders.

Thus do we learn that a good action is never thrown away, and that kind words and patient love will overcome the harshest natures.

ROBERT JONES BURDETTE

EXPLOSIVE IN THE TREE

So No. 3 Cmdo were very anxious to be chums with Lord Glasgow so they offered to blow up an old tree stump for him and he was very grateful and he said dont spoil the plantation of young trees near it because that is the apple of my eye and they said no of course not we can blow a tree down so that it falls on a sixpence and Lord Glasgow said goodness you are clever and he asked them all to luncheon for the great explosion. So Col. Durnford-Slater DSO said to his subaltern, have you put enough explosive in the tree. Yes, sir, 75 lbs. Is that enough? Yes sir I worked it out by mathematics it is exactly right. Well better put a bit more. Very good sir.

And when Col. D. Slater DSO had had his port he sent for the subaltern and said subaltern better put a bit more explosive in that tree. I don't want to disappoint Lord Glasgow. Very good sir.

Then they all went out to see the explosion and Col. DS DSO said you will see that tree fall flat at just that angle where it will hurt no young trees and Lord Glasgow said goodness you are clever.

So soon the[y] lit the fuse and waited for the explosion and presently the tree, instead of falling quietly sideways, rose 50 feet into the air taking with it ½ acre of soil and the whole of the young plantation.

And the subaltern said Sir I made a mistake, it should have been 7½ lbs not 75.

Lord Glasgow was so upset he walked in dead silence back to his castle and when they came to the turn of the drive in sight of his castle what should they find but that every pane of glass in the building was broken.

So Lord Glasgow gave a little cry & ran to hide his emotion in the lavatory and there when he pulled the plug the entire ceiling, loosened by the explosion, fell on his head.

This is quite true.

FROM *THE LETTERS OF EVELYN WAUGH*, EVELYN WAUGH

BARON MUNCHAUSEN
DANCES THE HORNPIPE

I embarked at Portsmouth in a first-rate English man-o'-war, of one hundred guns, and fourteen hundred men, for North America. Nothing worth relating happened till we arrived within three hundred leagues of the river St Lawrence, when the ship struck with amazing force against (as we supposed) a rock; however, upon heaving the lead we could find no bottom, even with three hundred fathom. What made this circumstance the more wonderful, and indeed beyond all comprehension, was, that the violence of the shock was such that we lost our rudder, broke our bow-sprit in the middle, and split all our masts from top to bottom, two of which went by the board. A poor fellow, who was aloft furling the mainsheet, was flung at least three leagues from the ship;

but he fortunately saved his life by laying hold of the tail of a large seagull, who brought him back, and lodged him on the very spot from whence he was thrown.

Another proof of the violence of the shock was the force with which the people between decks were driven against the floors above them: my head particularly was pressed into my stomach, where it continued some months before it recovered its natural situation.

Whilst we were all in a state of astonishment at the general and unaccountable confusion in which we were involved, the whole was suddenly explained by the appearance of a large whale, who had been basking, asleep, within sixteen feet of the surface of the water. This animal was so much displeased with the disturbance which our ship had given him (for in our passage we had with our rudder scratched his nose) that he beat in all the gallery and part of the quarterdeck with his tail, and almost at the same instant took the main-sheet anchor, which was suspended, as it usually is, from the head, between his teeth, and ran away with the ship . . .

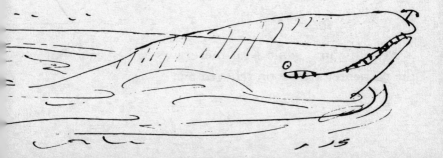

While the whale was running away with the ship, she sprang a leak, and the water poured in so fast, that all our pumps could not keep us from sinking; it was however my good fortune to discover it first. I found it a large hole about a foot diameter; and you will be glad to know that this noble vessel was preserved, with all its crew, by a most fortunate thought! In short, I completely filled it with my posterior, without taking off my small-clothes, and indeed I could have done so had the hole been larger still. For I am commonly considered to be somewhat broad in the beam.

My situation, while I sat there, was rather cool, but the carpenter's art soon relieved me.

I was once in great danger of being lost in a most singular manner in the Mediterranean: I was bathing in that pleasant sea near Marseilles one summer's afternoon, when I discovered a very large fish, with his jaws quite extended, approaching me with the greatest velocity; there was no time to be lost, nor could I possibly avoid him. I immediately reduced myself to as small a size as possible, by closing my feet and placing my hands also near my sides, in which position I passed directly between his jaws, and into his stomach, where I remained some time in total darkness, and comfortably warm, as you may imagine.

At last it occurred to me that by giving him pain he would be glad to get rid of me: as I had plenty of room, I played my pranks, such as tumbling, hop, step, and jump, and so on, but nothing seemed to disturb him so much as the quick motion of my feet in attempting to dance a hornpipe; soon after I began he put me out, by sudden fits and starts: I persevered; at last he was discovered by the people on board an Italian trader, then sailing by, who harpooned him in a few minutes. As soon as he was brought on board, I heard the crew consulting how they should cut him up, so as to preserve the greatest quantity of oil. As I understood Italian, I was in most dreadful apprehensions lest their weapons employed in this business should destroy me also; therefore I stood as near the centre as possible, for there was room enough for a dozen men in this creature's stomach, and I naturally imagined they would begin with the extremities: however, my fears were soon dispersed, for they began by opening the bottom of the belly. As soon as I perceived a glimmering of light I called out lustily to be released from a situation in which I was now almost suffocated. It is impossible for me to do justice to the degree and kind of astonishment which sat upon every countenance at hearing a human voice issue from a fish, but more so at seeing a naked man walk upright out of his body: in short, gentlemen, I told them the whole story, as I have done you, whilst amazement struck them dumb.

After taking some refreshment, and jumping into the sea to cleanse myself, I swam to my clothes, which lay where I had left them on the shore. As near as I can calculate, I was near four hours and a half confined in the stomach of this animal.

FROM *BARON MUNCHAUSEN*
RUDOLPH ERIC RASPE

CAPTAIN CAP AND THE
WONDERS OF FLIGHT

_____

There are few occupations that I enjoy more than sitting in some well-chosen Parisian drinking establishment with my much-travelled friend Captain Cap, and listening to his conversation. On this occasion, however, I have to admit that I was beginning to be bored with all his talk of balloons, of flying machines, of gliding machines, and goodness knows what else of the kind. In fact I was just on the point of inventing some excuse for leaving when a robust-looking gentleman, who seemed to have been taking a lively interest in Cap's grand notions, got up and came across to us. He formally offered an extremely elegant visiting card on which were the words:

SIR T. FIABLE

WINNIPEG

Now, we love Canada, Cap and I, and meeting a Canadian, even an English Canadian, always fills us with delight. So, it was with a welcoming smile that we greeted this noble stranger and invited him to join us for a drink. Once we had exchanged the pleasantries so necessary

to polite society, Sir T. Fiable said, 'The thing is, I happen
to know a bit about ballooning. A long time ago I did it
in what were perhaps unique conditions, never equalled
the world over!'

I saw Cap raise the shadow of an eyebrow ... *Conditions never equalled the world over!* ... Here was a rash
foreigner indeed!

Nothing daunted, Fiable continued, 'The interesting
thing about my ascent was that *I* was the balloon.'

When he had thoughtfully had our glasses replenished, Fiable continued, 'It was about ten years ago . . . I was captain of the brig *King of Feet*, loaded with sulphuric acid and bound for Boogletrout. One night at the mouth of the St Lawrence we were neatly sliced in two by a great steamer of the Dark Blue Moon Line and we sank to the bottom, crew, cargo, the lot.'

'Tragic.'

'You're right. It was rather tragic. As it happened I was wearing my sealion-skin boots, waterproof admittedly, but not really the thing for breaking any swimming records in. I was lucky enough to stay afloat for a moment on a stray oar. However, in the end, numb with cold, I followed the example of my ship and crew and I sank. But, and here's the thing, I managed to keep my sangfroid, and I had a clear plan in my head of what I had to do.'

'What a cool customer!'

'I most certainly was: all this took place at the end of December.'

'Highly amusing, sir.'

'With the heel of my boot, I broke off a piece of metal from the hull of my brig and, having crumbled it between my powerful fingers, I gulped the whole lot down. As I was at that time most unusually strong, I grabbed hold of one of the sunken jars of sulphuric acid and swallowed a few mouthfuls.'

'All this at the bottom of the sea?'

'Yes, sir, all this at the bottom of the sea. You're not always in a position to choose your laboratory. Well, you can guess what happened next, can't you?'

'We can, but explain it anyway for the benefit of those of our readers who are unfamiliar with chemistry.'

'Quite so! Every time iron, water and acid come into contact, hydrogen is given off. All I had to do was to keep my natural orifices hermetically closed, especially my mouth, and after a few seconds, filled with the precious gas, I rose to the surface. However, I must admit that I had miscalculated the strength of the gas. Not only did I float, I rose into the air and was carried along upstream by a rather brisk easterly breeze. At first, this

244

new sport delighted me, but after a while the charm of it wore off. And so, at daybreak, I opened the corners of my mouth very slightly as one does when one smiles. A little hydrogen escaped; slowly, I regained my normal weight and soon I landed in a very pretty little town called Gulldroop, just at the mouth of the Saguenay River. Do you know Gulldroop?'

'I should say we know Gulldroop! There's that pretty old church. And those girls who sell photos of the church – they're rather pretty too . . .'

After this slight intervention, the gentleman from Winnipeg finished his story with a relaxed air that was almost insulting to poor old Cap.

'The moment I set foot to earth, I exhaled what little hydrogen I still had in me and I set off for the Gulldroop salmon farm, singing that romantic old French song that I love so much:

> Leave the roses to the roses
> And the elephants to the Lord Mayor . . .'

Captain Cap was obviously irritated. He shrugged his shoulders and said in a rather loud whisper, 'There's something about this chap that strikes me as not entirely serious.'

ALPHONSE ALLAIS

THE PROFESSOR STUDIES
SPRING CLEANING

Professor Branestawm was having his breakfast in the bathroom. Of course, that was the sort of thing Professor Branestawm was always rather likely to do, through thinking about professorish sorts of things instead of about breakfastish sorts of things. But that wasn't the reason this time. Mrs Flittersnoop, his Housekeeper, had started spring cleaning, and all the other rooms were being turned out.

'Spring cleaning is silly,' said the Professor to himself, spreading marmalade on the sponge and wondering why it tasted funny. 'I must speak to Mrs Flittersnoop about it, I must.'

Just then Mrs Flittersnoop came in to see if he wanted some more toast, and was just in time to stop him trying to crack a piece of soap instead of his egg.

'Begging your pardon, sir,' she said, 'but I was wondering if you'd be going out rather earlier this morning, as I'd like to be getting on with the cleaning like so as to get it done with, if I might make so bold.'

'Not at all,' said the Professor, pouring himself out a cup of tea, but pouring it into the bath by mistake instead of into his cup, so that it all ran away goggle goggle, uggle oof, down the waste pipe. 'That is to say, of course, yes, yes, I'll be getting along now.'

He took a bite out of a rather crisp piece of toast which burst into crumbs all over him, and went downstairs.

Downstairs was all full of furniture, for all the rooms were being turned out at once, so that everything was everywhere, with one or two things left over.

'Dear me,' said the Professor. He'd forgotten about the spring cleaning on the way downstairs, and he thought he must have walked into a furniture shop or something.

'I'll take this,' he said, picking up a chair that he rather fancied. It was the one he always sat in when he wanted to think, so no wonder he rather fancied it. 'Just wrap it up for me, will you.'

'Yes, sir,' said Mrs Flittersnoop, who had come downstairs behind the Professor. She hadn't the least idea why he wanted his chair wrapped up, but the Professor often wanted things done she had no ideas about, so she just took the chair and wrapped it up as best she could, which was very badly, and left most of the chair showing.

'Er, thank, you,' said the Professor, looking at her over the top of two pairs of glasses and underneath the other three pairs. Then picking up the chair he went out in his slippers, because he'd forgotten to change into his boots, and got on a bus to go and see his special friend Colonel Dedshott of the Catapult Cavaliers. But he had the most severe sorts of trouble with the chair on the bus, which was nearly full. Some of the people thought he had stolen it. Some of them thought he was taking it to mend, because what they could see of it sticking out of the wrapping certainly looked as if a few spots of mending wouldn't hurt it. Others thought he wanted to sell it and buried their noses in their newspapers or stared at the advertisements in the bus or pretended to be looking for their handkerchiefs, in case he should ask any of them to buy it. One rather large gentleman, who'd been standing fourpennyworth already and was getting tired, thought he'd brought it on for him to sit on. So he sat on it and the Professor got off at the top of the Colonel's road and forgot all about the chair, which had goodness knows how many pennyworths of free ride and finished up in the Lost Property Office.

'Ha!' said the Professor, as he rang the bell. 'Dear old Dedshott. Quite a time since I saw him. Must ask him round to tea.'

Just then the Colonel himself opened the door,

because his two butlers, ex-Catapult Cavaliers, were out
in the garden beating a carpet with the rolling-pin and
a coal shovel. Professor Branestawm was busy at the
moment writing down a note on his cuff to ask the
Colonel to tea, and he walked straight in without seeing
the Colonel at all. And the Colonel, not being used to
opening doors himself; had opened it right back on himself and was trying to get away from the coat and the
hat pegs which were sticking into him slightly. So he
didn't see the Professor come in. They hunted about for

each other all over the place, but as the Colonel didn't know it was the Professor who had called, the Professor had to do most of the real looking.

At last they ran into each other, back to back, outside the coal shed.

'Ah! my dear Dedshott,' said the Professor, holding out his hand to shake hands, with the pencil he had been making notes with still in his fingers.

'Branestawm,' said the Colonel, in a warm sort of voice, for he was glad to see the Professor. He gripped the pencil by mistake for the Professor's hand. The Professor let it go, put his hand in his pocket and said, 'Can you lend me a pencil?', took his own out of the Colonel's hand, forgot what he was making notes about anyway, and they both went inside to have a glass of something.

'You must excuse things being so messed up,' said the Colonel, after they had had two cups of something, because the Colonel couldn't find the glasses, 'we're

spring cleaning, and some of the rooms are being turned out. It's an awful nuisance,' he went on, 'having to turn all the things out of a room and then turn them all back again. Why don't you invent a machine that will do it?'

'What say?' asked the Professor, who had been trying to work out how many times 3785 went into $8978756453645263555\frac{7}{8}$ or something on the tablecloth, but had come to the edge before he had finished.

'I say, why don't you invent a machine to turn rooms out and then turn them back again,' said the Colonel, getting out the laundry book and adding 'one tablecloth' to the other things on the week's list. 'It would make things so nice and easy.' The Colonel understood all about domestic things like that. He could even mend his own socks, though he never did.

'Wait a minute,' said the Professor, excitedly emptying the Colonel's cup instead of his own, which was already empty, and starting to think like anything. 'I see what you mean. A sort of machine or engine of some kind connected as to its differentials by a crank operating in inverse ratio to –'

'Yes, yes,' cried the Colonel, not understanding any of what the Professor was saying, but knowing he'd go on and on until his head went round and round, which he didn't want it to do. 'I think you have the idea all right.'

But Professor Branestawm wasn't listening to the Colonel. He'd started to invent his spring-cleaning

machine and nothing else mattered, not even if it did. He forgot about the Colonel, he forgot he was in the Colonel's house and not in his own, and started taking a clock to pieces to get out some special kind of little cog-wheels he wanted for his machine.

So while the Professor was busy with his inventing, the Colonel thought he would slip over and tell Mrs Flittersnoop not to bother with any more spring cleaning, as the Professor's machine would do it all for her as soon as he got it invented, which probably wouldn't be very soon, but never mind. Well, he certainly slipped over all right, but that was because he trod on a piece of orange peel, and by the time he got to the Professor's house the cleaning was all done and the furniture all back in its place, except the chair the Professor had taken away; that was still at the Lost Property Office.

'Well,' said Mrs Flittersnoop, when she heard about what the Professor was doing, 'that will be nice I'm sure, not having to turn the rooms out. A thing I never could abide. And seeing as how the Professor's staying with you, sir, as it were, perhaps you'd be so kind as to give him his boots, sir, which same he left behind him this morning.'

'Oh – er, yes, not at all, certainly,' said the Colonel, taking the boots in one hand and raising his hat with other other. 'Er – good day.'

'Good day to you, sir, I'm sure,' beamed Mrs Flittersnoop. 'Such a nice gentleman,' she said to herself as she went back to the kitchen to send a note to her sister Aggie to say she'd stay with her for a bit, which she always did when the Professor was away, for company or something.

'Good Heavens!' exclaimed Colonel Dedshott when he got back to his house. 'Whatever has happened? Accident? Explosion? Awful, terrible, oh dear!' The house was in a simply extreme muddle. Everything was everywhere except a few things that seemed to be nowhere. The piano was upside down in the coal cellar. The dining-room chairs were in the garden. The large picture of the Colonel in his Catapult Cavalier's uniform was all in bits, thank goodness, for it looked awful. Some of the carpets were up the chimney, and one chimney, at least, seemed to be all over the carpet. The gas cooker had a knot in the middle of it, and the best silver was wrapped in the spare-room mattress.

'Oh! my goodness me and all,' wailed the Colonel, coming all unmilitary at seeing his nice house all over the place. 'What has happened, and why and how? Shall I go and fetch the police or the fire brigade or the old-iron man or what?' He rushed into room after muddled-up room looking for the Professor, but couldn't find him. He found a chair just inside the kitchen door by falling over it. He found that the bath had got turned inside out, and when he struck a match to be able to see better, he found a slight escape of gas, and *voilà*! down came considerable ceiling. But the Professor was nowhere to be seen.

The Colonel was just going to rush out screaming when something dark and dirty, and wearing five pairs of spectacles, issued from the umbrella stand. It was

Professor Branestawm. Good gracious!

'I fancy some of my calculations were a little inaccurate, my dear Dedshott,' he said. 'I just had the machine nearly finished and something went sort of whiz and here I am.'

'Yes, I see you am – I mean, are,' said the Colonel, ramming his hands into his pockets so hard he burst clean through the bottoms of them, and sent fivepence halfpenny and four bull's-eyes spinning all over the floor. 'But here you don't stay. You just go home and invent your own house to bits, will you. I ought to have known better than let you stay here alone after what happened to the clock-man's house over the never-stop clock.'

'I – er, I – er,' began the Professor.

'Yes, I know you err,' said the Colonel, getting all clever for a moment. 'That's just the trouble. Go home and err there, that's a good chap.'

So the Professor went home and got there just at the same moment as a man from the Lost Property Office who had found some papers with the Professor's address in the stuffing of the lost chair, and had brought it back. So he gave the man his hat and left twopence on the hallstand instead of the other way round. But the man was a bit quick-witted through doing crossword puzzles, and he changed them over, otherwise the Professor's hat might have gone into the Lost Property Office.

Then the Professor had a nice hot wash and started inventing the spring-cleaning machine all over again, while the Colonel had men and people in to put things right. It cost him an awful lot, but, fortunately, the Colonel had simply pyramids of money left him by some fancy aunties or someone, so it didn't matter very much.

At last the machine was finished, but not before several entirely unreasonable things had happened, such as the Professor forgetting what he was inventing and turning it into a new kind of mangle that would do nearly every-thing except mangle, and then getting caught up in bits of invention and having to shout for Mrs Flittersnoop to get him out, which, fortunately, she was able to do because she had come back from her sister's and she did knitting a lot and understood tangles.

'There you are,' said the Professor to Colonel Dedshott, whom he had asked over for tea to see the machine. 'No more bother with spring cleaning. You just push this button and pull that lever and twiddle these wheels, one one way and one the other, then, at the same time, you lift this up here and pull that and adjust the –'

'Lovely,' said the Colonel hurriedly before his head began to go round and round as it always did when the Professor started explaining things. 'Let's have a go with it.'

They carried it upstairs and put it in one of the rooms. 'Now when I start it,' said the Professor, 'it will turn everything out of the room, and then clean all the dust out without us doing anything. You watch.'

He twiddled and pulled and pushed and turned and lifted up this, that, and the other.

'Bz-z-z-z-z-pop, bang, chug-a-chug,' went the machine, and they ran out to watch it work.

'Pop, pop, bang-a-chug, bz-z-z-z, whizz, squee-eeeeeow, op,' went the machine.

The Professor, the Colonel, and Mrs Flittersnoop ran out and stood in rows in the garden.

'It isn't going to work,' snorted the Colonel, wondering if it was tea-time yet.

Just then a nicely rolled-up carpet came sailing out of the window and fell on him.

'Ah!' said the Professor, and then a bed fell on him. A wardrobe missed Mrs Flittersnoop by inches, goodness knows how many, but it didn't matter because it was a special one of the Professor's own invention and made of rubber, so it wouldn't have hurt anyway.

'There you are,' said the Professor, coming out from under the bed just in time to be hit by a pillow. 'What

did I say? There's your spring cleaning being done, Mrs Flittersnoop.'

'Indeed it is, sir,' said Mrs Flittersnoop, getting behind a bush in case any more wardrobes were coming. 'Wonderful, I call it, these things coming out like that.'

Soon everything that had been in the room was in the garden, but still the machine went on popping and clicking and whizzing.

'I'll go and stop it,' said the Professor. He ran upstairs and the next minute he came sailing out of the window and landed in the geranium bed, but, fortunately, all the geraniums had been scratched up the week before by Mrs Flittersnoop's sister's dog who was staying with them.

'Stop it!' gasped the Professor, with his mouth full of geranium bed.

'I'll stop it,' shouted the Colonel, and in he ran, followed by Mrs Flittersnoop and the next-door man, who had come over the fence to see what was doing.

The next minute they all came out of the window together and fell on the special rubber wardrobe, which burst with a slight pop, scattering the Professor's spare socks, some books, a pot of jam, a small saw, a half-invented clockwork draught-board, but no men, and a piece of toffee that the Professor had kept there.

'Gracious,' gasped the Professor, rushing round the geranium bed, which, luckily, happened to be a round one. 'I see what it all is, I do. That machine was made to turn things out of a room and it keeps doing it. Whenever anyone goes in to stop it, it turns them out. What can we do, good gracious, don't ask me.'

'But it must be stopped,' shouted the Colonel, and in he dashed again, but out he came again. Seven times he tried to stop that awful machine and seven times it threw him out. The geranium bed was full of dents.

The Professor fetched all the Great Pagwell Police, but the machine threw both of them out. He got the Fire Brigade, the Gas Company, and the Pagwell Borough Council, and it threw them out, all except the Mayor of Pagwell, who hadn't come in case it wasn't dignified.

'Oh dear! oh dear!' groaned the Professor, getting all his five pairs of spectacles so mixed up that he was seeing long-sighted sorts of things through his near-sighted glasses. 'Oh! I don't believe I'll ever invent anything else if I can remember not to.'

'Look here,' said the Colonel, 'we can't let that thing go on chugging and whizzing and throwing people out like that. Something absolutely has got to happen about it and happen soon, I tell you.'

Just then something did happen about it. The machine itself came out of the window and fell with such a rattle in the geranium bed that three crocuses came up long before their time.

'Heavens!' gasped the Professor, guessing what had happened, because he knew more about the machine than the others, but not much more. 'It's turned itself out, so it has.'

'Well I never,' said Mrs Flittersnoop, but nobody minded whether she ever or not. They were all too busy looking at the machine and saying things they didn't understand themselves to show how clever they were.

'Now,' said the Professor, 'I will show you how the machine puts things right after turning everything out of the room including all the dust and itself.'

He pulled a pushed lever. He untwiddled a twiddled wheel and he left several other things alone. Immediately the machine rose in the air and went back through the window.

'See!' cried the Professor, dancing about with excitement, 'now it will take the things back.' Which that wonderful machine proceeded to do. The bed and the chairs and the carpet and all the other things went sailing back through the window.

'Wonderful!' gasped everyone, but the next minute they none of them knew where they were until they found themselves packed into the rather small room in which the machine stood.

'Help!' shouted the Professor from between three firemen, Colonel Dedshott, and two Borough Councillors. 'It's turned us in.'

It certainly had and it didn't stop there, for in through

the window came clouds of dust, half-bricks, pieces of this and that.

'Stop! Stop!' shrieked the Professor, as everyone rushed for the door and got stuck half-way. 'It'll bring the whole of everything here in a minute.'

Suddenly there was a crash and things stopped coming in. The garden roller had come in with the other things and landed right on the machine, smashing it to bits.

With a last despairing chug the spring-cleaning machine was finished.

'Thank goodness for that,' said everyone, mopping their foreheads with one another's handkerchiefs which they'd taken from one another's pockets by mistake because they were so crowded up.

They got themselves sorted out at last and went outside while Mrs Flittersnoop made cups of tea. Then everyone went home, feeling that a good, if exciting, time had been had by all.

Mrs Flittersnoop had to do all the spring cleaning over again because of the mess the machine had brought in. But the Professor let her have her sister Aggie's two aunties in who were both very good at cleaning, so it didn't take so long.

FROM *THE INCREDIBLE ADVENTURES OF
PROFESSOR BRANESTAWM,*
NORMAN HUNTER

GOLDFISH IN EVERY BEDROOM

When I was head aquarium keeper at Boulton Wynfevers, the commodious Tudor residence of the seventeenth Baron Shortcake, we had goldfish in every room. 'Travers,' my master would say to me, 'have you changed the fish-water in Lady Katharine's room?' or, 'Travers,' he would call from the minstrels' gallery, 'are the fish in the Hon. Guy Clobbock's room eating well?' or, 'Travers,' he would yell from the gunroom, 'the fish in Lady Muriel's boudoir are making so much damned noise I can't hear myself eat.'

We had one fish that snored, and we always put it in Lord Thwacker's room, and told him it was the ghost of the ninth baron . . .

Towards his eightieth year my dear old master became an even greater goldfish-addict than before. He filled the house and grounds with goldfish, and I, as head aquarium keeper, was often called to flick the fish off people's clothes, or to drive them from the dining-hall table.

One evening, when sprats Melba were on the menu, Lady Thrashurst ate six sleeping goldfish by mistake. They had crept on to her plate. The consciousness of her error brought her to her feet with a roar of shame and anguish, and so energetically did she wriggle and squirm as the rudely awakened fish struggled in her throat that my master, recalling the Eastern dances of his youth, shouted an Oriental oath and clapped his hands.

On the morning after my old master had lost £73,000 in IOUs to a guest, we sold the entire Boulton Wynfevers collection of goldfish to a lonely old lady who had just cut her niece out of her will. From that day the Baron changed. He would wander listlessly from room to room, calling the absent fish by name and starting guiltily if he thought he saw a movement in the empty bowls.

He would sit late at his dinner, and would often call for me to repeat some story of the fish, saying, 'Travers, tell them about that time when two Burmese Rovers got

down the back of Lady Felspar's dress,' or, 'Travers, do you recall how that little devil Silver Slipper drank a glass of my Meursault on the night of the fire?' or, 'Travers, I do not think Sir Arthur knows the story of how Tiny and his gang got into the Bishop's hot-water bottle and tickled his feet.' And he would sigh and say, 'Those were the days.'

They were, indeed, the days. Once a year the grounds were thrown open to the villagers and their friends, and the London papers would send photographers and reporters. The Baron was usually photographed standing between two of the biggest bowls, and little girls dressed as goldfish would curtsy to him and present him with an album in which to stick snapshots of his favourites and prizewinners.

Twelve years running we won the Shires Cup for the smartest turn-out, and the fish always got fresh water and an extra meal – not to mention a playful flip on the back from the beaming owner.

I still treasure the photograph of myself standing between my master and Lady Mockett and holding up Jellaby Wonder II by the tail.

Deafness troubled my old master considerably towards the end of his life. I remember an occasion on which he was entertaining the Lord Lieutenant of the County to dinner. He, also, was deaf. He suggested to Lord Shortcake that the craze for tropical fish was dying out.

'By topical,' said my master, 'I presume you mean fashionable.' 'I don't agree,' rejoined the Lord Lieutenant. 'I think they are unfashionable. They are aliens in any aquarium.' 'Who are aliens?' asked my master. 'No, no,' said the Lord Lieutenant. 'Not us. I said the fish.' 'Damn it,' hotly retorted Shortcake, 'what fish are you talking of?' 'No, no,' said the Lord Lieutenant, 'not us. I said the fish.' 'What?' roared my master. 'Do you mean *all* fish?' 'Well, they *are* all fish, aren't they?' said the Lord Lieutenant angrily.

As the evening wore on and the port in the decanter sank lower and lower, the two deaf men groped for an understanding. When the Lord Lieutenant spoke of flying fish, my master thought he had said 'frying fish'. He grew enraged at the idea of frying valuable specimens of his collection. 'But surely,' said the Lord Lieutenant, 'you keep flying fish?' 'I do no such thing,' replied Shortcake, 'and if I did I should do it in the kitchen, not in the aquarium.' 'That's the first time,' said the Lord Lieutenant, 'I ever heard of anybody with an aquarium in his kitchen.' 'Besides,' said my master, 'you couldn't eat most of them, even if you fried them.' 'There you are!' said the Lord Lieutenant, 'what's the good of flying fish?'

Nothing annoyed Lord Shortcake more than an obvious indifference to his goldfish. He would say to a guest before retiring, 'You will find your bowl in your room. Don't disturb the fish more than is neccesary.'

The tactless guest would sometimes grin and say nothing or even show surprise, as though he were unused to such a thing. But what my dear master liked was to get some such reply as, 'Oh, but how very thoughtful of you! What breed are they? How many? What age? Certainly I will not disturb them.'

On one occasion a young lady of title, on receiving the parting information and admonition went into screaming hysterics, which infuriated my master. 'Does she think they are mice?' he asked me several times.

On another occasion a stupid dowager cried, 'What! Real goldfish?' 'Have you ever seen goldfish that weren't real?' snapped my master. 'But, do you mean *real* goldfish, like the ones in bowls?' she continued. 'Damn it all, madam,' said my master, 'I don't know what kind of

goldfish you have been used to, but there's no nonsense about mine.'

'But why in the bedroom?' asked the dowager. 'Why on earth not?' countered Lord Shortcake. 'What odds is it to them what room they are in?' 'Well, I shall put them outside the door,' said the dowager. 'You can do that with your boots, but not with my fish,' said my master. 'Why not,' he added, 'fill your boots with water and put them in the bowl with the fish instead?' The dowager considered this for a while, and then left the room in high dudgeon.

I would not like my readers to have the idea that life

at Boulton Wynfevers was all goldfish. There were days when my master became profoundly dissatisfied with his hobby. 'Travers,' he would say to me, 'these damned fish never *do* anything. They roam round their bowls, but anybody can do that.'

It was my task on such occasions to comfort him by referring to the sheen on their coats, or their efforts to look intelligent when shouted at, or their value as ornaments. 'Bah,' he would say, 'I prefer a good bloater. You can, at any rate, *eat* a bloater.' I would then point out that you can't keep bloaters in bowls all over a house. 'Quite right, Travers,' he would say, 'one must make allowances.' And he would add, 'It takes all sorts to make a world.'

Curiously enough, my old master was always afraid of fire destroying his fish. An Indian law student had once told him that goldfish are terrified of fire. That is why, during the winter, their bowls were always placed as far from the fires as possible. And he even asked the chief of the local fire brigade to submit a plan for dealing with an outbreak of fire among the fish. This gentleman said, 'Oh, but they're safe enough. They're in water.' 'So are ships,' said the Baron, 'but they catch fire.' There was a fire-alarm in every room, and I, as head aquarium keeper, had to wear a fireman's helmet and carry an axe on windy days . . .

My dear old master was of so kindly a nature that he was easily victimized. He was asked once to stand for

Parliament, the member for the constituency having died. On his inquiring what they would like him to stand as, a go-ahead member of the local football club said, 'Why not the Goldfish candidate? Better treatment for our dumb friends, and all that. Good publicity value.'

My old master replied that goldfish were not dumb. He said they mewed very faintly, at certain seasons. Otherwise, he said, he was prepared to present the case for better treatment for all fish to the representatives of the nation ...

Among my duties at Boulton Wynfevers, as I have stated, was the counting of the goldfish. Every night, before the household retired to bed, I had to hand to my dear old master a slip of paper with the total figure written on it.

The figure was always 13,874, since every dead fish was replaced at once, from a reserve tank, by a living one. But Shortcake always took the thing seriously. He would say, 'Hum! 13,874. Not bad, Travers, not at all bad, eh?'; or, 'By George, Travers, 13,874, did you say? Pretty sound figure, eh?'; or, 'Bravo, Travers, we're keeping it up, eh?'

Once I wrote 13,847 by mistake, and my dear old master made me count them all over again. 'Slippery little devils,' he kept on saying. 'Can't be too careful.' . . .

My late lamented mistress, Lady Shortcake, who died in 1938, had often been accused of feigning interest in goldfish in order to keep my old master in good humour. But is it likely that any lady of her attainments could have stooped for sixty-one years to such deceit? The only member of the family who actively disliked the fish was the third son, Stanley. 'There must be some bad streak in the boy,' my old master would say. 'It isn't natural. He's not a Shortcake.' His own excuse, that he was bitten by a Yellow Peril in boyhood, was never taken seriously at Boulton Wynfevers. 'Pah,' my master said once. 'If they were only bigger I'd put my head in their mouths without a tremor.'

The thought of Lord Shortcake with his head in a goldfish's mouth was too much for one of the young butlers. His chest heaved with inward laughter, and an entire dish of peas, about to be offered to Lord Hoopoe, slithered down the ear-trumpet of the Dowager Lady

Garment, who had just placed the instrument in position in anticipation of some outrageous compliment from her neighbour. The cascade of peas against her leathery old ear drew from her an eldritch shriek. 'She might have awakened the fish,' said my master calmly, when it was all over, and she had apologized to Lord Hoopoe for smacking his face.

Aubyn Spicecraft, my dear old master's secretary, was one of those secretaries who must fold a newspaper before handing it to anybody, so that it has to be unfolded again before being read. This, he said, gives an employer the idea that he is independent and can look after himself. That is why, he would say, employers always unfold newspapers so pompously.

Lord Shortcake was interested only in stories about goldfish. If there were none in the papers, he sent them out to the servants' hall. It was Mr Spicecraft's task to mark with a blue pencil any such stories, and then to cut them out and file them after my master had read them. In addition to this, we subscribed to a press-cutting agency, which sent us all references to goldfish.

It was Spicecraft, of course, who took down at dictation and typed my dear old master's monumental work, *A History of Japanese Crossbreeds*, in eight volumes, with coloured plates of every kind of odd goldfish known to mankind. I cannot resist quoting its closing words, which hang above my Aquarium-Keeper's Diploma as I write. 'And so, reader, we say farewell to goldfish. May everybody find such constant companions upon life's thoroughfare as I have found. For this world is but a bowl, where we poor mortals blunder round and round until our brief day is done. Nor, with all man's boasted brains, can he rival in beauty the little fish which has been the subject of my humble work. Gentlemen, I give you the toast: Goldfish!'

FROM *LIFE AT BOULTON WYNFEVERS*,
J. B. MORTON

THE WASP IN A WIG

A very few steps brought Alice to the edge of the brook, and she was just going to spring over, when she heard a deep sigh, which seemed to come from the wood behind her.

'There's somebody *very* unhappy there,' she thought, looking anxiously back to see what was the matter. Something like a very old man (only that his face was more like a wasp) was sitting on the ground, leaning against a tree, all huddled up together, and shivering as if he were very cold.

'I don't *think* I can be of any use to him,' was Alice's first thought, as she turned to spring over the brook: 'but I'll just ask him what's the matter,' she added, checking herself on the very edge. 'If I once jump over, everything will change, and then I can't help him.'

So she went back to the Wasp – rather unwillingly, for she was *very* anxious to be a Queen.

'Oh, my old bones, my old bones!' he was grumbling on as Alice came up to him.

'It's rheumatism, I should think,' Alice said to herself, and she stooped over him, and said very kindly, 'I hope you're not in much pain?'

The Wasp only shook his shoulders, and turned his

head away. 'Ah, deary me!' he said to himself.

'Can I do anything for you?' Alice went on. 'Aren't you rather cold here?'

'How you go on!' the Wasp said in a peevish tone. 'Worrity, worrity! There never was such a child!'

Alice felt rather offended at this answer, and was very nearly walking on and leaving him, but she thought to herself 'Perhaps it's only pain that makes him so cross.' So she tried once more.

'Won't you let me help you round to the other side? You'll be out of the cold wind there.'

The Wasp took her arm, and let her help him round the tree, but when he got settled down again he only said, as before, 'Worrity, worrity! Can't you leave a body alone?'

'Would you like me to read you a bit of this?' Alice went on, as she picked up a newspaper which had been lying at his feet.

'You may read it if you've a mind to,' the Wasp said, rather sulkily. 'Nobody's hindering you, that *I* know of.'

So Alice sat down by him, and spread out the paper on her knees, and began. '*Latest News. The Exploring Party have made another tour in the Pantry, and have found five new lumps of white sugar, large and in fine condition. In coming back –*'

'Any brown sugar?' the Wasp interrupted.

Alice hastily ran her eye down the paper and said 'No. It says nothing about brown.'

'No brown sugar!' grumbled the Wasp. 'A nice exploring party!'

'*In coming back,*' Alice went on reading, '*they found a lake of treacle. The banks of the lake were blue and white, and looked like china. While tasting the treacle, they had a sad accident: two of their party were engulphed –*'

'Were *what?*' the Wasp asked in a very cross voice.

'En-gulph-ed,' Alice repeated, dividing the word into syllables.

'There's no such word in the language!' said the Wasp.

'It's in this newspaper, though,' Alice said a little timidly.

'Let it stop there!' said the Wasp, fretfully turning away his head.

Alice put down the newspaper. 'I'm afraid you're not well,' she said in a soothing tone. 'Can't I do anything for you?'

'It's all along of the wig,' the Wasp said in a much gentler voice.

'Along of the wig?' Alice repeated, quite pleased to find that he was recovering his temper.

'You'd be cross too, if you'd a wig like mine,' the Wasp went on. 'They jokes at one. And they worrits one. And then I gets cross. And I gets cold. And I gets under a tree. And I gets a yellow handkerchief. And I ties up my face – as at the present.'

Alice looked pityingly at him. 'Tying up the face is very good for the toothache,' she said.

'And it's very good for the conceit,' added the Wasp.

Alice didn't catch the word exactly. 'Is that a kind of toothache?' she asked.

The Wasp considered a little. 'Well, no,' he said: 'it's when you hold up your head – *so* – without bending your neck.'

'Oh, you mean stiff-neck,' said Alice.

The Wasp said 'That's a new-fangled name. They called it conceit in my time.'

'Conceit isn't a disease at all,' Alice remarked.

'It is, though,' said the Wasp: 'wait till you have it, and then you'll know. And when you catches it, just try tying a yellow handkerchief round your face. It'll cure you in no time!'

He untied the handkerchief as he spoke, and Alice looked at his wig in great surprise. It was bright yellow like the handkerchief, and all tangled and tumbled about like a heap of sea-weed. 'You could make your wig much neater,' she said, 'if only you had a comb.'

'What, you're a Bee, are you?' the Wasp said, looking at her with more interest. 'And you've got a comb. Much honey?'

'It isn't that kind,' Alice hastily explained. 'It's to comb hair with – your wig's so *very* rough, you know.'

'I'll tell you how I came to wear it,' the Wasp said. 'When I was young, you know, my ringlets used to wave –'

A curious idea came into Alice's head. Almost every one she had met had repeated poetry to her, and she thought she would try if the Wasp couldn't do it too. 'Would you mind saying it in rhyme?' she asked very politely.

'It aint what I'm used to,' said the Wasp: 'however I'll try; wait a bit.' He was silent for a few moments, and then began again –

> 'When I was young, my ringlets waved
>   And curled and crinkled on my head:
> And then they said "You should be shaved,
>   And wear a yellow wig instead."
>
> But when I followed their advice,
>   And they had noticed the effect,
> They said I did not look so nice
>   As they had ventured to expect.

They said it did not fit, and so
    It made me look extremely plain:
But what was I to do, you know?
    My ringlets would not grow again.

So now that I am old and gray,
    And all my hair is nearly gone,
They take my wig from me and say
    "How can you put such rubbish on?"

And still, whenever I appear,
    They hoot at me and call me "Pig!"
And that is why they do it, dear,
    Because I wear a yellow wig.'

'I'm very sorry for you,' Alice said heartily: 'and I think if your wig fitted a little better, they wouldn't tease you quite so much.'

'*Your* wig fits very well,' the Wasp murmured, looking at her with an expression of admiration: 'it's the shape of your head as does it. Your jaws aint well shaped, though – I should think you couldn't bite well?'

Alice began with a little scream of laughter, which she turned into a cough as well as she could. At last she managed to say gravely, 'I can bite anything I want.'

'Not with a mouth as small as that,' the Wasp persisted. 'If you was a-fighting, now – could you get hold of the other one by the back of the neck?'

'I'm afraid not,' said Alice.

'Well, that's because your jaws are too short,' the Wasp went on: 'but the top of your head is nice and round.' He took off his own wig as he spoke, and stretched out one claw towards Alice, as if he wished to do the same for her, but she kept out of reach, and would not take the hint. So he went on with his criticisms.

'Then your eyes – they're too much in front, no doubt. One would have done as well as two, if you *must* have them so close –'

Alice did not like having so many personal remarks made on her, and as the Wasp had quite recovered his spirits, and was getting very talkative, she thought she might safely leave him. 'I think I must be going on now,' she said. 'Good-bye.'

'Good-bye, and thank-ye,' said the Wasp, and Alice tripped down the hill again, quite pleased that she had gone back and given a few minutes to making the poor old creature comfortable.

LEWIS CARROLL

INDEX OF AUTHORS

ACKNOWLEDGEMENTS

The editor and publishers gratefully acknowledge the following for permission to reproduce copyright material in the form of short stories and extracts in this book:

'The Liquorice Tree' by Joan Aiken from *The Winter Sleepwalker and Other Stories* published by Jonathan Cape, copyright © Joan Aiken, 1994, reprinted by permission of Random House UK Ltd; 'Captain Cap and a Musical Interlude' and 'Captain Cap and the Wonders of Flight' by Alphonse Allais, translated by Quentin Blake, English translation copyright © Quentin Blake, 1996; Extract from *The Letters of Evelyn Waugh* ed. by Mark Amory, published by Weidenfeld & Nicolson, copyright © The Estate of Laura Waugh, 1980, reprinted by permission of The Orion Publishing Group Ltd; 'Maggie McWhistle' by Noel Coward from *A Withered Nosegay*, published by Christophers 1922, copyright © 1922, The Estate of Noel Coward, reprinted by permission of Reed Consumer Books Ltd by arrangement with Michael Imison Playwrights Ltd; Extract from *Charlie and the Chocolate Factory* by Roald Dahl, published by Penguin Books Ltd, copyright © Roald Dahl Nominee Ltd, 1964, reprinted by permission of Murray Pollinger; 'Seven Shopping Days to Christmas' (extract) by Clement Freud, from *Grimble* and *Grimble at Christmas*, published by Penguin Books Ltd, copyright © Clement Freud, 1968, 1974, reprinted by permission of Mark Paterson and Associates on behalf of Sir Clement Freud; 'The Little Mouse, the Little Bird and the Fried Sausage' by the Brothers Grimm from *Tales from Grimm: retold by Ulla Dolt and Geoffrey Summerfield*, published by Ward Lock. 'The Love Story of a Spud' by Pierre Gripari from *Contes de la Rue Broca*, reprinted by permission of Editions de la Table Ronde, Paris, English translation by Quentin Blake, English translation copyright © Quentin Blake, 1996; 'Father Crocodile's Christmas High' and 'Christmas at Aunt Fidget Wonkham Strong's' by Russell Hoban from *The Times Educational Supplement 19th December 1980* copyright © Russell Hoban, 1980, reprinted by permission of David Higham Associates; 'Living in W'Ales' by Richard Hughes from *The Spider's Palace* published by Penguin Books Ltd, reprinted by permission of Random House UK Ltd and David Higham Associates; Extract by Norman Hunter from *The Incredible Adventures of Professor Branestawm* published by The Bodley Head, copyright © 1933, The Estate of Norman